Miss Nackawic
Meets Midlife

Colleen Landry

Chocolate River Publishing would like to acknowledge the support of the New Brunswick government and the New Brunswick Book Fund's literary book promotion program for the support of their publishing program.

Library and Archives Canada Cataloguing in Publication

Landry, Colleen, author

    Miss Nackawic meets midlife / Colleen Landry.

ISBN 978-0-9959384-3-4 (softcover)

      1. Middle age--Humor. I. Title.

PS8623.A5156M57 2018   C818'.602   C2018-903305-3

Printed and bound in Canada

Chocolate River Publishing
PO Box 7092
Riverview, NB
E1B 4T8
www.chocolateriver.ca
chocolateriverpublishing@gmail.com

Miss Nackawic Meets Midlife

Colleen Landry

Chocolate River Publishing
www.chocolateriver.ca

In memory of my mom,
Carolyn Roy,
who relied on Erma Bombeck's humour to survive motherhood.
I'd like to think that this book too, would make her laugh.

Early reviews

Literally the best book in the universe—super hilarious! Five thumbs up!
   —*Miss Nackawic 1981*

I busted a gut! OMG, this author makes the word 'the' funny!!
   — ~~Ellen~~ *Colleen Landry*

~~Mom wrote a book?~~ A masterpiece!!
   —*Alex Landry*

 I love ~~shepherd's pie~~ this book!!
   —*Max Landry*

My wife is a friggin' ~~wingnut~~ genius!!
   —*Phil Landry*

Colleen was a ~~defiant~~ creative child and it was clear from Day 1 she would
be a total ~~headcase~~ success. This amazing bestseller proves it.
   —*Ron Roy*

ACCORDING TO *Page 2, Section A, Subsection 5F* of my worn out copy of the *Beauty Queen 101 Handbook*, a piddly 1% of the population has (legally) worn a tiara and sash 24/7 for an entire year. Guess what, you guys? I'm among the ~~elite~~ blessed few to be in that 1% (My thoughts and prayers go out to those in the 99% who are searching for their life's purpose—it must totally suck). Thirty-six years ago, I literally beat the odds...I became *Miss Nackawic 1981*. You heard me—I reigned over the town of Nackawic, NB, for ~~491~~ 365 days. Let that sink in for a minute. A beauty queen wrote the book you are holding. For reals.

My path in life literally changed on that awesome September night in 1981. Before I became royalty, I wasn't sure what I wanted to be when I grew up. It's not that my future wasn't bright—I mean, I was on a bowling team that finished in seventh place, and I was a solid C (ish) student—obviously I could have done anything with my life! Duh. It's just that I wasn't sure I wanted to be a professional bowler and yea...my marks were beyond outstanding, but what was the point of university?? Nah. I wanted something more, and once I felt that cold, ~~diamond-encrusted~~ shiny tiara dig into my feathery bangs I knew what that *something* was—winning *Miss World* and total fame! Boom. The universe had spoken and I was listening. According to *Page 2, Section A, Subsection 5F.2* of the *Miss World* handbook, only 0.000000001% of former beauty queens go on to become Miss World, but I intended to beat the odds again. I had the passion and the personality ~~disorder~~ to go all the way to the top, obviously. All I needed was the right pair of sandals and *Miss World* would ~~never ever~~ be mine for the taking. It felt amazing, at the age of sixteen, to finally have a meaningful purpose!

Since chances are you've never been in, much less won a pageant, I'd like to give you a behind-the-scenes glimpse into what it's really like. Close your eyes and imagine it's September 3, 1981, the night of the Miss Nackawic pageant. The arena is packed to the rafters with ~~a custodian~~ plain, regular people, desperate to find out who their new ruler will be. The lights on the stage are blinding and hot, and I'm standing there in my homemade pink, sheer(ish) chiffon gown, wishing I'd worn underwear. Whatever. A bead of sweat trickles down my cheeks, giving me an awesome dewy glow. I silently congratulate myself on my talent portion—an air guitar routine. I know deep down I nailed it even though I was super dizzy from swinging my head so much. I pray that the last-minute cartwheel I almost landed during the evening gown catwalk pays off for me—I did it to show my spontaneity, which is the fifth most desirable trait in a beauty queen according to *Page 15, Section B, Subsection 3C* of the handbook. Boom.

Next comes the interview portion. My question is: *Should more businesses be wheelchair accessible?* I answer: *Duh. There should definitely be more businesses in Nackawic because I have to drive all the way to Fredericton to shop for shoes and that's totally unfair!* Nailed it. The judges go off to make their decision. The wait feels like twelve million years. Finally, the Master of Ceremonies walks toward the microphone. I'm so nervous I literally almost black out. The pressure makes me wish I was in the audience with the plain people. I take a deep breath. The M.C. opens the judges' envelope and lets out a funny sound like a dying animal would make. (Weirdo) He shakes his head, shrugs his shoulders, and then says literally the best words I've ever heard in my entire life: "Um. This is a joke right?? Well, if you saaayy so... *Miss Nackawic 1981* is Colleen Roy."

The flashes from ~~my parents~~' the paparazzi cameras blind me. I'm literally attacked by ~~my parents~~ the press as they bombard me with praise and questions. At one point, they even bow before me. That's when things get real—I'd waited my entire life for proof that I was better than everyone, and, when the people bowed, I knew it was true! I was literally the Chosen One and in that instant I knew I was made for a life of waving at peasants, wearing pretty gowns and riding on parade floats.

Can I be honest? After that night, I fully expected my life to spin out of control, but everyone in my town was terrified I'd end up like one of those child-actors-turned-cokeheads, so they really ~~ignored me~~ respected my time and space. I was too young to understand it at the time, but, looking back, I'm actually relieved I didn't explode to stardom and turn into a diva. Instead, it was more of a ~~delusion~~ slow burn. I literally shudder to think of what those Hollywood overnight-success kids go through. Back to me now...

This book is my gift to you and the dreamer inside you. It's the story of a small-town, sixteen-year-old girl with big hair and even bigger dreams—a girl who blossoms into a ~~wrinkly~~ stunning, middle-aged(ish) woman who wants more out of life ~~but never gets it~~. It's the story of one girl's vision ~~board~~ and her extreme ~~delusion~~ perseverance when faced with ~~reality~~ over three decades' worth of roadblocks. You too, can have what I have—a future filled with ~~dirty laundry and Hamburger Helper~~ hope that your big dream is just around the next corner.

Put your seatbelt on and enjoy the ride ~~at my expense~~. I hope this book makes you feel a whole lot ~~better about your life~~ of emotions. I think it will. I also hope you paid a minimum of $40 for it, because I have bills to pay. Wait. What?? Fourteen dollars and ninety-five measly cents is all you put down for this masterpiece?? Dear Publisher: You're fired! Wow. Somebody owes me some friggin' money.

September, 1981

Dear Miss World Pageant Organizers:

I'm sure by now you've heard that I won the title of
Miss Nackawic, NB last night!! I was chosen as the best
person in my entire town, and I honestly deserved it.
It was literally the best night of my life. ~~My parents~~
The paparazzi went nuts and took a whole bunch of pic-
tures. I'm literally famous!! EEEEEEEEE!!

Here's me right after they announced my name:

Even though some people yelled,
"It's been rigged. There's no way
in hell…!" I just held my head
high like royalty does under pressure. Then, as I got up from my
chair to accept my jewelled tiara,
the other two girls in the pageant
mumbled very rude things and I got
flustered and tripped and by mistake I crushed their feet with my
sensible beige Kmart sandals (because we had no money for fashion-

able sandals, that's why!!) I felt terrible about it,
but sometimes royalty must literally step on people.
It's just the way the world works. Not my fault.

I plan to take my ~~rain, reighn,~~ title very seriously. I
know there will be challenges like how the heck will I
know who my real friends are now? Frig. I'm just going
to be super ~~vigalinte, vigilint~~ careful. For example,
when my BFF asks me to come over to watch <u>Another</u> <u>World</u>
and eat a six-pack of strawberry Pop Tarts, I'll be all
like "Is it 'cus you want to borrow my tiara??" Whatever. No one said this would be easy.

When Miss Nackawic 1980 placed that shiny tiara on my
head, it was wicked awesome and I finally knew what I
wanted to do with my life—become a full-time beauty
queen, obviously. Dear high school guidance counsel-

lor: Thanks, but no thanks to those dumb career fairs!! Working for a living sounds totally boring. Ha! Ha! Plus, my other dream of becoming a pro athlete/Olympian didn't work out because, apparently, you need to be an expert and practise more than twelve hours/year before you can even get a shot at the pro world. Who has THAT kinda time?? Frig that. All I need is a shiny tiara, a sash, and five totally hot bodyguards, and I'll be on my way!! A life of staring into a camera and waving at people is what I want!!!

That's where you come in. Now that I'm a beauty queen, I am ready to put Nackawic on the map and become Miss World. You heard me. Miss World 1982 is mine for the taking, but first I need to know where it's being held next year. Also, how do I apply for this ~~presteegous prestigius~~ totally tubular position??? I want this sooooo bad, you guys!!!!!

Please mail me back or call me at:

(506)769-2589 (ROY-ALTY)

Sincerely,

Colleen Roy
Miss Nackawic 1981

PS Will the gown be provided? I'm thinking something simple, but with a 12-foot train. I'm a size 8. Thank you!

PPS Will there be a swimsuit competition? That would be super gnarly! I'm seriously hot (Insert sizzling sound).

September 1982,

Dear Miss World Pageant Organizers:

I'm sure you're wicked busy these days getting ready for the pageant, which is probably why I didn't hear from you last year. Whatever. Um, I think I got ahead of myself when I wrote to you guys anyway. I wanted to jump right from <u>Miss</u> <u>Nackawic</u> to <u>Miss</u> <u>World</u>, but I didn't realize I had to win <u>Miss</u> <u>New</u> <u>Brunswick</u> first!! Duh. Ha! Ha!

I was stoked when I found out I would be ~~Miss New Brunswick 1982~~ representing my hometown on the provincial stage!!! The pageant was held in Woodstock, NB, so I had to leave home for a week. I quickly found out that the road to stardom isn't always easy—it was totally awful to be in a place where I wasn't recognized everywhere I went. Apparently people in Woodstock don't read newspapers, or they would have seen my picture splashed over the front page a year ago. Whatever. Another thing that happened was I got a super moody roommate. She was obviously threatened by my awesome feathery bangs because she barely spoke to me! I guess I'd be jealous of me too, so I just let it go and focused on why I was there—to win Pageant #2! Boom.

In the end it turned out to be a total waste of a week!! I didn't win Miss ~~Stupid~~ NB, but it wasn't my fault. As *if*. Get this: The judges were looking for someone with perfect skin, shiny blonde hair and a ~~dumb~~ talent for pitch-perfect singing! Gag me with a spoon! Plus, there were ten girls in the pageant! Ten!!! Oh, and the pageant organizers told us to "just be yourself" which was terrible advice because I spent the entire week goofing around and making fun of the dance instructor behind her back. If I'd known it would affect my chance at the title, obviously I would have been more ~~demyour damure~~ fake. Not my fault.

Beauty queens don't give up though! I've learned my lesson, and I won't make the same mistakes on your stage. To prove it, I'll have you know I've enrolled in Miss Manners' Finishing School at the local college. Plus, I'm working to fix my split ends, which I'm sure had something to do with me losing, but it wasn't my fault the hotel didn't provide conditioner. The pageant winner had shiny blonde hair, so I'm assuming she brought conditioner from home, which is basically cheating, but whatever.

Here's the problem: My parents say I need to start applying for university (Blah. Blah. Blah.), but I have bigger dreams. University is for total losers, and studying is hard work. Frig that. Please send me information on how to apply for Miss World, so I can start preparing ASAP.

Sincerely,

Colleen Roy
Miss Nackawic 1981

PS Will my expenses be paid? That would be totally awesome 'cus I'm super broke.

PPS I'd prefer my own room with a king size bed, but I will accept a queen size. Get it?? QUEEN...that's me. Ha! Ha!

September 1983

Dear Miss World Pageant Organizers:

Hello again!! I'm sure you remember me from the two other letters I sent. Jeepers. I wonder if I have the address right?? I find it weird that you haven't gotten back to me. Oh well... I'm not goin' anywhere. I am reeaally ~~delusional~~ patient. Don't you worry. Ha! Ha!

I just wanted to let you know what's going on in my life, so you can update your files. Are you sitting down?? I'm at university... because the application deadline was coming up... and I STILL HADN'T HEARD FROM YOU, so my parents forced me to apply. They said it would be good for me to spread my wings and move out on my own (Blah. Blah. Blah.) and that they needed my bedroom for a TV room. Pfft. I didn't like my room anyway so there.

Okay, I'll admit it, you guys. University is totally awesome! I'm having so much ~~beer~~ fun, but, when I'm out in public, I can assure you I represent myself in a regal fashion. When I dance on the tables in a wet T-shirt, I keep it clean(ish). Even though it's a blast, I want you to know that I plan to quit university the minute you RESPOND TO MY MAIL. But, for now, my parents are insisting I "be practical" and "become a teacher." Ha! Ha! Very funny. I've got bigger plans than that, thank you very much. All I need is for you to GET BACK TO ME at your earliest convenience... or by the end of next week. That would be even better. Please try, okay?
Thank you sincerely,

Colleen Roy
Miss Nackawic 1981

PS What is the age cut-off for Miss World?

PPS What is the average waist size of previous winners? Please say 29 inches.

September 1989

Dear Miss World Pageant Organizers:

Yo! Wassup? It's been a while and a half. Holy! Who knew university would be more than just dancing on tables and distributing Miss Nackawic Forever bumper stickers? Frig! I actually had to write essays and study—sometimes both in the same week which explains why I've been out of touch. Please accept my sincere apologies for making you worry about me. You'll be thrilled to know I'm alive and well and the fire in my belly for Miss World is literally burning a hole in it! Ha! Ha! Although my life looks perfect on the surface, beneath my tiara and sash is that sixteen-year-old beauty queen with big hair and big dreams still waiting patiently for that big break. At times it feels like I'm talking to a wall, but I know these things just take time, right, you guys?

Update alert: I live in Toronto now (Is the pageant held here?) and I teach kindergarten. My parents think they're so smart and that just because when I was a kid I played teacher 24/7 and bossed my friends around that teaching is my calling. They're wrong. Oh sure. . .I'm obviously making a massive difference in the world, one child at a time—it's precious when they follow me around like the paparazzi and tell me I'm prettier than their mothers ~~or they don't get recess~~ but I will drop them like a hot potato WHEN YOU GET BACK TO ME.

Once I hear from you, I will submit my letter of resignation to my principal and focus on what really matters—perfecting my catwalk strut, finding the perfect gown, and practising my best surprised look and acceptance speech. Here's what I looked like the night I won Miss Nackawic 1981—it's pretty good but I think I can do better and use more body language.

Mainly I need to know where the pageant is being held!!
I honestly DON'T KNOW HOW MUCH LONGER I CAN WAIT for
Miss World 199* —and the obvious spinoffs: my very own
bodyguards, clothing line, and signature fragrance.
Just kidding! Duh. I'll wait forever to wear the <u>Miss
World</u> tiara! Give me a shout and we can discuss the
juicy details. I'm stoked!

Sincerely,

Colleen Roy
Miss Nackawic 1981

PS I watched <u>Miss World 1989</u> last night and noticed
they all have a talent. Should I be concerned about
this? Do I absolutely <u>need</u> a talent? Frig.

PPS I put on five(ish) pounds because there are so many
awesome restaurants in Toronto you wouldn't believe it!
My bad. Serious diet starts tomorrow!!!!!!! Promise.

To: missworldpageant.com
Subject: Call me!
October 10, 1992 at 1:00 AM

Dear MWPO:

Three years since my last letter! Wow, time sure flies when you're ~~wasting your f#$%ing life~~ having fun! Ha! Ha! Please note I have email now. This will make things much easier for you to get back to me in a timely manner—no stamp—no envelope—no fuss—and I will no longer lie awake wondering if you received my ~~#$%ing~~ letters. I hate to point fingers, but if my email to you shows as *Sent*, and I don't hear from you it means the problem is on your end so…

Since you're dying to know I'll spill it—I'm married now to a super awesome and hot guy!!! You heard me. The wedding was a week ago!! My last name is now 'Landry'. Can you please make a note of that so you will recognize that it's me in future correspondences? Thank you.

Being a stunning bride was amaaazzzing, and it made me feel like royalty all over again. It gave me a taste of the glamour that awaits me when I take the title of *Miss You Know What*. Wink. Wink.

Here's a picture of me and my sweet, handsome husband, Phil, on our wedding day.

Oops! Here's the real one. Ha! Ha!

I was blinded by the ~~hired photographer~~ paparazzi as I walked down the aisle. My husband was confused when I chose to wear my *Miss Nackawic 1981* sash over my gown, but it was simply to show everyone **that I am more than a gorgeous, awesome wife**. Duh. I have depth. Let's just say, he'll be happy about the sash decision when I take home the million dollars along with the crown. The prize *is* a cool 'mill' right?? Could you clarify this for me please? I'm still going to go for it, but it would help with our tight budget if I could factor this in. Should I cancel the inground swimming pool?? Please advise ASAP—the backhoe arrives on Wednesday!

Sincerely,

Colleen Landry
Miss Nackawic 1981

PS I'd like my husband to be my escort on pageant night. Is that okay or will you provide me with someone? Will that someone be Brad Pitt?

PPS I'm now a size 6 because I lost weight for my wedding! I'm ready for the bikini portion of the pageant. Boom.

To: missworldpageant.com
Subject: Helloo??? Anybody there??
September 1, 1999 at 4 p.m.

Dear Miss World Pageant Organizers:

Greetings from suburbia where my dream of becoming *Miss World* is ~~dying faster than that stupid #$%ing herb wreath Martha Stewart promised would grow~~ front and center, even though I'm crazy busy and in love with my ~~temporary~~ situation! I'm still a teacher and wife and homemaker, but there is no doubt I was meant for fame and royalty.

Guess what else, you guys??! I'm a mother! You heard me. A few years ago, I gave ~~up my perfect figure~~ birth to two totally perfect boys with perfect names—Alexander and Maxim!! Swoon. When my darling babies looked into my eyes for the first time, it was love at first sight. I felt bad that the glare from my tiara made them squint, but they had to get used to it at some point. I won't pretend childbirth was my best look—my hair was all damp and stuck to my head, and let's just say that horse stirrups are more regal than the kind I had to jam my freshly pedicured feet into… Furthermore, waterproof mascara does not—I repeat—does not work during labour. It ran down my face, and, by Hour #10, I looked like a homeless cokehead. But being seen in such an unglamorous light was worth every bad hair and makeup day times a million, because my boys are literally perfect! Childbirth was hell though, and I looked like total crap. Did I mention that?

Here are my royal heirs adjusting to the glare from my tiara

Can I level with you? I thought raising kids would be a cinch because on those sitcoms, there are only a few little problems in each episode and they always get resolved during the half hour show. I'm here to tell you it's not like that at all! I have tried making our boys watch sitcoms so they understand the thirty-minute wrap-up rule, but they just run from me screaming, "No TV!! Want cookie!" OMG. Plus, they want me to read to them and build towers with blocks. WTF. That is why I sometimes literally go days without so much as a full-body massage or a perfectly foamed latte—so you can imagine how hard it has been to work on pageant-related stuff much less write to you!

Also, unlike sitcom toddlers, mine are quite self-absorbed which is super hard for me to deal with because I'm just not like that—I'm all about shining the spotlight on others. My boys don't understand the art of conversation. For instance, rather than asking *me* questions, they ramble on about their hopes (Kraft Dinner for lunch) and fears (the dark, loud noises, no Kraft Dinner for lunch), but heaven forbid I share *my* hopes and dreams. The second I plunk them in front of the TV to watch the recorded *Miss World* 1981-1998 pageants, they cry and whine, "No queen! Want cookie!!" See what I deal with?? I'd like five friggin' minutes with a sitcom writer—they're obviously totally whacked in the head.

This brings me to the purpose of this email. Are you guys sitting down? Sigh. It deeply pains me to inform you that I have no choice but to remove myself from the *Miss World* eligibility list and fully devote myself to raising these adorable boys. It takes time to teach children what matters in life— assembling the perfect playground outfit, getting prepped for a photo shoot and walking with a book on their heads to prepare for the catwalk—and unfortunately, I am the only one who can provide that for them. Trust me—this is just a pause because, as I've said before, *Dreams don't go away. They fester until you die* ~~which I hope you do face down in a gutter~~.

Sincerely,

Colleen Landry
Miss Nackawic 1981

PS When I do (and I will. Boom.) resume my quest for *Miss World*, should I aim for **Mrs**. *World*? Be honest, you guys.

To: missworldpageant.com
September 21st, 2003 at 6 AM
Subject: I'm ba-aack!
Dear Miss World Pageant Organizers:

Hi guys! I'm ba-aack! What's your screen name on MSN so we can connect in real time? Mine's Miss Nackawic 1981—duh—and remember…no blocking allowed!! Ha! Ha! Guess what? I'm literally 'this close' to pursuing the title of *Miss World* again because our precious boys are in school! You heard me. They are no longer toddlers who cry and whine for me to stop shining my 'tiawa' and play with them 24/7. Needless to say, I'm glad those days are over!

Can I be honest with you though? I thought when our boys became a bit older that maybe life would get easier, and I'd have tons of time to pursue my other dream. I still don't know how those people on sitcoms do it!! Their houses are dreamy, their kids are colour-coordinated and rarely place each other in headlocks. Frig. I just don't get it.

The other thing that bugs me is I'm also still teaching full time. That wasn't how it was supposed to be, remember?? I should be riding on floats, waving to regular people, and accepting bouquets. At the very least, I should have had my own fashion line by now. I still have my letter of resignation tucked inside my top drawer at school, but I hate to submit it before I hear from you because I need the cash. Houses are super expensive. Who knew?

I'm ready to go hard at my dream again, so I guess I'll have to get my priorities straight and make the commitment. If that means quitting the *Home and School* committee, skipping parent/teacher interviews, and ignoring our children after 6 p.m., so be it. You may not like what I'm about to demand, but I see no other option. If I'm willing to basically quit parenting, then you have to do your part to ensure my future win. Here are some non-negotiable requirements, you guys:

•   Personal chef—There is no way in hell I have time to cook meals and practise walking around the house in a bikini and stilettos. Impossible.

•   Housekeeper—I can't have a clean house and recover from a tummy tuck. Those two things shouldn't even be in the same sentence.

•   Cognitive therapist—This is to help me to cope with the trappings of fame obviously. I can't afford it on a teacher's salary. Enough said.

Don't worry—I'm worth the investment. In my spare time, after recovering from the tummy tuck, I plan to do my part. You guys have my total word that I will:

- Buy a new wardrobe, complete with glittery gowns for all seasons—since I don't know what time of ~~mother #$%ing~~ year I'll be competing.

- Keep my hair freshly highlighted—so I'm ready to go at a moment's notice.

- Get Botox every six months even though I hate needles—sacrifice is my middle name.

- Redo my kitchen in case the interview is via Skype—duh, I need a decent backdrop.

Spoiler alert: That list literally overwhelms the crap out of me, not to mention that it will take most of our nest egg! UGH!! I can't just give up now though! I have to cling to my mantra in tough times like this: *A winner is just a loser who tried one more time*, according to Mr. Know it All, George M. Moore Jr.

Sincerely,

Colleen Landry
Miss Nackawic 1981

PS Are pedicures covered in the pageant?? My feet look like something straight out of *The Hobbit*.

PPS Would a one-piece bathing suit be okay for the bikini portion just in case I can't afford a tummy tuck?

PPPS I've started a crowdfunding campaign to help with the tummy tuck costs—$27 so far! Boom.

To: missworldpageant.com
Subject: I'm on twitter now. Follow me you guys.
September 1st, 2008 at 2AM
Dear Miss World Pageant Organizers,

Hashtag hello!! Is it a firewall issue that kept you from accepting my
#$%^ing Facebook friend request? No worries. Since I'm totally hip, (the
thirty-ninth most desirable trait in a beauty queen according to *Page 16,
Section B, Subsection 3C* of the handbook) I'm on Twitter now! Have you
heard of it? It's super easy. I'll follow you and you follow me and together
we can make this thing happen. My Twitter handle is @missnackawic1981.

Here are some tweets I've already put out into the cyberweb thingy to show
you how serious I am about dominating your pageant!! Please retweet
them and answer my questions using the chat bubble picture thingy.
Hashtag I can't wait to win!

@missnackawic1981 2008-09-01 Miss World here I come! Please retweet
    #royalty

@missnackawic1981 2008-09-02 Anyone know where Miss World 2008 is
    being held?? #privatemessageme

@missnackawic1981 2008-09-03 Can't wait to represent the entire uni-
    verse in 2009!! Please retweet!

@missnackawic1981 2008-09-04 Does anyone know a cheap plastic sur-
    geon? #privatemessageme

@missnackawic1981 2008-09-05 Free Miss Nackawic bumper sticker for
    first 100 followers! #uheardme

@missnackawic1981 2008-09-06 I have a dream!!–Miss Nackawic 1981
    (and MLK) #whatever

@missnackawic1981 2008-09-07 Patience is a virtue! #desirable #trait #67

@missnackawic1981 2008-09-08 I took a little fall today–stilettos snagged
    on carpet. #swollen #ankle

@missnackawic1981 2008-09-09 Bedazzling vision board while recovering
    from ankle injury #can't #stop #me

To: missworldpageant.com
Subject: You didn't keep your end of the bargain!!
September 6th, 2012 at 3 AM

Dear Miss World Pageant Organizers:

Hi guys!! I'm baaaaccck! Life has been super busy and time is literally zipping by. Can you believe I have teenagers now?? You heard me. Those precious little boys have grown into fine young men who are hungry all the time, but they only eat when they're awake, thank God. They don't chit chat ~~at all~~ as much as they used to, but I know they still love and totally admire me. Obviously.

Also, I gave up on the sitcom thing—I figured out after Family Meeting #472 that they wanted nothing to do with those perfect thirty-minute wrap-ups. They liked to keep things real, which meant I did some unglamorous stuff for several ~~@#$ing~~ years—picking up wet towels, grocery shopping, cooking supper, driving our boys all over the place, and making endless ~~threats~~ lunches.

It's been super exhausting and at times I literally want to hang my~~self~~ head and cry, but I needed to stay strong so I could keep up with my ~~mother~~ ~~@#$ing~~ chores!

I have something else to say—you guys did not provide me with the support staff I requested (personal chef, housekeeper and cognitive therapist) years ago! Since you didn't keep your end of the bargain, I backed out of mine and decided to continue parenting and being an amazing mom. Because of that, I had no time to focus on the pageant! Grrrr!

This process feels literally endless, but, to be honest, I'm glad I didn't quit *Home and School* or parent/teacher interviews or *Microwave Mom* because that plaque the principal gave me still hangs proudly in my bedroom: *Helicopter Parent 2009.* Boom. It's good to be involved in your kids' lives, obviously.

Despite being an awesome mother, wife and ~~slave~~ organizer of everything, I still picture myself on a parade float waving to the ordinary people. That mental image plus a healthy dose of ~~Cabernet Sauvignon~~ chutzpah (pronounced *hootzpaw* obviously) are what get me through the rough days.

I'll have you know the minute I pick up the last soggy towel and drive our awesome boys to their last hockey game, I'm totally yours! You heard me.

It's super exciting to think I've still got what it takes and that even decades of family life can't distract me from what's rightfully mine. I'll be in touch soon. Promise!!

Sincerely,

Colleen Landry
Miss Nackawic 1981

PS Will you provide the wine or should I bring my own crate?

September 4th, 2015

Dear Miss World Pageant Organizers:

Boom. My second born baby boy left for university and I'm totally fine with being ~~a washed up nobody~~ alone. Pfft. Hardly even noticed when my loinfruit up and left me for whatever reason. It's a bit of an adjustment getting used to my new life without them, but, for now, driving by the boys' university residence and blowing kisses just feels right. I know they'd be thrilled if I went ~~away~~ full out for my dreams now, but I need them to know I still love them to the moon and back, and I still will after I become super famous. My hourly texts to them are obvious proof:

Hi precious little man! How is university? Are you okay ~~without me~~ with your new teachers? I was going through photo albums and found a picture of you eating strained peaches for the first time. Do you remember?? You LOVED them but made such a mess with them! Ha! Ha! I miss you. Do you miss mommy? xoxo

Hi precious little man! I haven't heard from you for a long time. Are you still in university? How tall are you now? Are you eating lots of vegetables? I found this picture of you eating ice cream for the first time. Do you remember?? You loved it but made such a mess! I miss you. Do you miss me? xoxo

Fine. Don't text me back. See if I care. Pfft. Guess I'm on my own—no more damp towels to pick up, no more meals to cook, no more ~~AA~~ school meetings. But in the quiet moments, I find myself oddly ~~drunk~~ paralysed with fear, you guys. Up to this point I've had totally legit reasons for not going after my second calling, but now I have to face the truth—I might be too old, or I might not be pretty or talented enough, or I might have wasted my entire life for nothing. Psych!! Ha! Ha! As if. Two words: I'm baaa-ck!

I'm putting away the old photo albums, pouring myself ~~into my skinny jeans~~ a glass of Shiraz, and embracing the next phase of life—fame and glory obviously. I know you guys are ~~idiots~~ shy about answering my letters, so I've taken it upon myself to write a detailed summary to show you how I've spent the last few decades. As you read it (tonight), please note how I've worked hard to excel at a variety of things to boost my chances at *Miss World*. Together, we can work to turn these everyday gifts into something I can bring to the world stage. If this doesn't meet your standards, then I will find ~~you and when I do so help me God~~ something else that satisfies your ~~stupid, impossible~~ criteria. I'm sure you'll be surprised at my ~~lack of~~ accomplishments and finally realize I am the best person to wear the *Miss World* crown. Boom.

Sincerely,

Colleen Landry
Miss Nackawic 1981

PS Has there ever been a winner with a moustache? Be honest, you guys.

PPS I'm a ~~liar~~ Size 6 ~~with arms that flap and wave when I stand still~~.

Section 1

We Were ~~Not~~ Just Like a TV Family

Bored Games

All I ever wanted was a TV family, complete with well behaved kids who played quietly for hours while I perfected my Smoky Cat Eye makeup look. Apparently, that was too much to ask. Instead, my boys chose to play loudly, throw things at each other, and constantly interrupt me, which is why to this day my eyeliner is super plain and doesn't have that cat-eye flair. Not my fault. Something had to change—I had to find a way to create my very own TV family with kids who got along and said stuff like, "May we please have more broccoli before our four-hour nap?" Well guess what? I found my answer while watching Season 3, Episode 7 of my favorite sitcom—the perfect children and their perfect parents were playing a board game after supper. It was totally civilized, and they said stuff like, "Your turn!" and "Awww, ya got me. Ha! Ha!" If they could do it, we couldn't do it. Boom. Right then and there I created *Family Games Night*. Obviously.

The next morning, I put my awesome plan into action. I interrupted the boys' wrestling match by putting them in ~~a headlock~~ the car and driving to Walmart to load up on—you guessed it—board games! It was hard to choose one because they all sounded super depressing: *Trouble, Taboo, Sorry!* Note to games makers: You don't make them sound fun at all. Pfft.

But some had 'Laugh out loud!' 'Guaranteed fun' and 'Even dysfunctional families love this one!' on the covers along with pictures of families who appeared to like each other. Sold! I loaded the games into the cart, located the bickering ~~devil~~ children in Aisle 5, peeled them off one another, and sashayed regally to the checkout.

After supper I hollered, "Hey, guys! Mommy wants us to be a perfect TV family! Come into the dining room for our brand new *Games Night!*" Their reaction was totally ~~dumb~~ unexpected. Instead of them running into my arms and thanking me for this awesome idea, they resisted.

Phil: Seriously?

Alex: I **hate** playing games.

Max: Me too. It's lame.

I rolled ~~a joint~~ my eyes and said, "C'mon guys. You ~~ruin everything~~ owe me this!"

They slumped in their seats, and the complaints started, "I want blue!!"

"It's taken. Besides, green is your favorite colour and you **know** it!" I scolded my whiny husband.

I put them in ~~another headlock~~ front of a bowl of popcorn and things ~~never~~ got better except for the butter stains that ended up on my favorite tablecloth. Whatever. These things probably happen to TV families too, so I just rolled ~~another joint~~ with it.

We made two teams. It felt like the boys didn't want to be on my team when they called out, "Boys against girls! Girls are weird." ~~Idiots.~~ Ask me if I care. The first game was over in under five minutes. My husband and Alex announced their win by high-fiving, fist-pumping and bragging, "We rule! You drool! Na! Na! Na! Na! Na!" Max turned against his TV family up-bringing, whipped the dice across the room, and said, "I quit!"

My husband rolled his eyes and said, "See? Games are not fun." Then they left me alone with my butter-stained tablecloth wishing like hell we hadn't just made the Kardashians look wholesome.

I ~~forced~~ suggested *Games Night* once more the following week. My non-TV family dragged themselves to the table again, and my husband gave me the ~~finger~~ dirtiest look on his way by. Whatever.

Alex: It's your turn. Go, idiot!

Max: Shut up and make me!

Phil: Why do you bother with this stuff?

Me: Let's make this a drinking game! I'll go first!

The wrestling match, name-calling, and ~~divorce threats~~ butter stains that followed made me wonder if I should just become an actor in a sitcom instead. It would be way easier. OMG. I gave up, threw those stupid games into the ~~garbage~~ hall closet, and never dug them out again. As far as I was concerned, having the perfect Smoky Cat Eye was more important than family bonding anyway. ~~Idiots.~~

30

Go Ahead. Shoot Me ~~Please~~

Before our boys grew up and left the perfect nest I'd created for them (Fine. Leave. See if I care. Pfft.), I wanted an updated, colour-coordinated, magazine-cover-worthy family photo. Apparently this was too much to ask—I quickly discovered that making love to the camera is **my** gift, not my handsome and totally camera-worthy sons' forte. For whatever reason, they hate wearing matching sweaters and shivering in the cold while I tell ~~the photographer to take ten years off me~~ them to scooch in closer and smile big for Mommy! As someone who always carries a fan, a wardrobe change, and her own portable backdrop, it's hard for me to understand their utter disregard for the pillars of our society—~~the paparazzi~~ photographers. I often think I should get a DNA sample to make sure these boys are even mine!! Honestly.

Not only do we feel differently about photo shoots, but we prepare super differently. Leading up to it, I had a bazillion things to do—get a haircut, my teeth capped, and a new ~~nose~~ wardrobe. On the day of the photo shoot, I ran around like crazy cleaning the house, ironing the matching sweaters, and calling ~~People magazine to see if they wanted first dibs~~ upstairs to tell the boys to wake ~~the hell~~ up. OMG, 'sleeping' and 'photo shoot' should never appear in the same sentence…like ever!

I waited until the fourth bowl of Froot Loops kicked in before I broke it to them, "~~Meet Lance. He'll be doing your hair and makeup.~~ It's pretty cold and windy out there, guys, and we can't wear jackets in the pictures." Then, I showed them their adorable matching sweaters.

One of them asked, "Uh. Where'd you get this, Mom?"

"Winners… Why?"

"It's a 'chick' shirt. There's no way I can wear this."

My husband ~~who will soon be available~~ said, "Ha! Ha! You look like a girl in that shirt." I instantly shot ~~my wedding ring down the toilet~~ him a deadly look while I showed the boys pictures straight from the pages of *Fashion Today* to prove the shirts were totally in vogue. They ignored me and changed into ~~dumb~~ non-matching shirts. To be honest, I felt like I was in this alone no matter how hard I tried to make it about them. Whatever. I had to rise above it, and I did that by setting up my portable backdrop, turning on my fan (for the tousled look obviously) and changing my outfit six ~~hundred~~ times.

When the photographer arrived, I told him I wanted ~~to be in PEOPLE magazine~~ authentic, natural shots. With the word 'authentic', the boys instantly relaxed. They stared blankly at their iPhones, cranked ~~each other in the head~~ the volume on *Cops*, scratched themselves, and burped.

Finally, it was show time! As we huddled and posed around an eyeball-sized spot on our front step, it became obvious that my family had refused to read my Power Point presentation on how to hide a double chin from the camera and smile with your eyes. They struggled with the simplest instructions and kept saying stuff like, "This is so lame." I reminded them that the words 'lame' and 'photo shoot' must never be spoken in the same sentence again as long as they both shall live! OMG. It felt like all my teaching had been wasted on them, and I silently vowed to stop airbrushing their school photos. Obviously they didn't care.

I literally pretended my ungrateful family wasn't even there, and I killed the rest of the shoot. The photographer seemed shocked with how natural I was and how far I could slither on the grass without hurting myself. Spoiler alert: I've done this before! Duh. It seemed the more ~~layers I removed~~ loose and alive I became, the more rigid my weird and uncooperative family became. Whatever. Plus, they whined about the weirdest things, like when the strong wind almost uprooted our maple tree. Who even cares?? You take the tousled look however you can get it…but not everyone in my family has my winning attitude, obviously.

After an hour of me ~~screaming, "This lighting is total crap! Get someone in here who knows what the hell he's doing!"~~ posing, I looked up for a split second and realized my family was gone! Then I spotted a note attached to the front door: *You obviously ~~are sick in the head~~ don't need us. Gone to football game.* Go ahead—be fickle and selfish. See if I care! To wind down the shoot, the photographer said, ~~"Work it, baby! You're incredible!"~~ "That'll be $200." And with that, it was over. I'd say the family photo was a success.

You be the judge:

Oops! My bad. Here's the airbrushed family photo which the photographer managed before they left me totally in ~~heaven~~ the lurch:

Oh, and speaking of judges, do we know who's judging *Miss World* this year??

My Boys Weren't Like Sitcom Teenagers When it Came to Mother's Day

Mother's Day was amazing when our boys were adorable pre-schoolers. I loved it so hard when they fought over who would serve me breakfast in bed while I fussed with my tiara and sash. They were super cute and their homemade cards made me weep with joy: *Mommy, yoo ar a kween. I luv yoo.* Swoon. What angels!! Then they would give me presents like kitchen forks, gummi worms, and potting soil. ~~WTF! I asked for diamond earrings!~~ It made me feel like a TV mom, and I honestly thought every Mother's Day would be like this—my one day/year of total fame.

It didn't work out that way because something terrible happened—they became teenagers! All of a sudden, they stopped ~~bowing~~ acknowledging me when I walked into a room and worse—I had to learn to read lips because they spoke in mumbles rather than words!! OMG, even when I said, "Use your words, sweetie!" they just ignored me. Pfft. Fine. See if I care.

My boys weren't like sitcom teenagers when it came to Mother's Day! First of all, they forgot that Mother's Day starts when the sun comes up, not at 1 p.m. when they woke up! Then they would drag themselves downstairs with iPhones in their hands, instead of presents for me. Whatever. After my husband nudged them and whispered, "Wish your mother a happy Mother's Day!!!" they would get finally get it and while staring at their phones, they'd say, *hpymrsdy,mom.* (Happy Mother's Day, Mom!) Then they said more beautiful things—*Wrstrvd* (We're starved).

I responded super lovingly, "I gave up my six-pack abs for you two ~~idiots~~ and the last time I checked, a six-pack is a requirement for *Miss World*!! In return, is it too much to ask that you behave like television people and honor your amazing mother in a way that would make my friends jealous?"

After that they decided to cook me breakfast. Once they located the kitchen, they looked to Phil for guidance. The questions they asked totally warmed my heart—*Whazzastove?* (What's a stove?), *Whassapan* (What's a pan?), *Wraregs?* (Where are eggs?). For the next two hours, they demonstrated their love for me by chopping, slicing ~~their fingers~~, and making instant coffee (WTF!! Where's my espresso and frothed 2% milk in a pre-heated pottery mug??). I was waiting for the piece de resistance—something I could post on Facebook to make other moms jealous…but it was taking a super long time.

When I noticed them slowing down in the kitchen and texting their friends, I tried to pump them up with a motivational speech—"I almost died giving birth!! I've never seen so much blood and gore but it was worth it to give you life and to have the privilege to cook and clean for you while my dreams sit on the back burner and speaking of which, the #$%ing bacon is on fire!" It seemed to help because they went right back to cooking! Hey, maybe my *Miss World* talent could be motivational speaker??

The pièce de résistance never came, but my breakfast did. It didn't make the Facebook cut, so instead I posted a picture of a breakfast I found on Pinterest with this message: *So blessed this Mother's day! Look at this feast my darling boys cooked for me…without being asked! Hoping all mothers out there are being treated like a queen today.*

After breakfast, the boys mumbled more thoughtful Mother's Day senti-ments—*See ya!*

I gently reminded them that on sitcoms, kids clean up their messes— *Where in the name of God do you think you're going? Maple syrup is dripping down the walls! I gave up my six-pack abs for you miserable little...!*

They did their whole "I'm deaf" thing and took off. Whatever. My one day of total fame was apparently a thing of the past. Just you wait until *they* become mothers. Pfft. I'll totally mess it up for them.

TV Families Make Halloween Look Super Easy

TV families always make Halloween look super easy and festive—their driveways are lined with jack-o-lanterns that don't resemble lopsided stroke victims; their kids' costumes are creative and people can even guess right away what they are; and their perfect children never throw up all over their beds from eating too much candy. It wasn't like that in my house when I was a kid—my mom bought me a plastic mask even though it came with suffocation warnings on the package; she put an orange light bulb in our front porch light (Ha! Ha! Kidding! She didn't), and I ate mini Kit Kat bars until I puked. I wanted more for my sweet boys, but, in the end, it turned out to be too much work, and I ~~gave up~~ decided to leave it to the braggart TV families. Pfft.

Costumes are hard. After years of putting a white hat on the boys' heads and telling them to just say 'Boo!' when people answered the door (Well it's better than the suffocation hazard I was forced to wear!!), I thought I'd died and gone to heaven when a ~~show-off~~ seamstress neighbour gave me two gently worn homemade costumes for our boys—one was a dinosaur and one was a panda bear. I was super grateful, and I passed them off as my own creations, obviously. Oh really?! You always tell the truth do you? Three cheers for the almighty archangel who does no wrong!!

Parading the boys around town in those awesome costumes ~~which I hand-stitched~~ year after year was my claim to fame. I was literally killing Halloween! Then two really bad things happened. They grew out of their costumes, and, even though I told them dinosaurs and panda bears look cute with short sleeves, they refused to wear them. Then a TV-mom impersonator moved in next door! She put as much effort into Halloween as I did preparing for *Miss World*. Get this—on October 30th, she brought over some treats she'd whipped up during her REM sleep phase—witches' fingers, jello eyeballs and a life-size candy corn scarecrow! She must have found out I was a contender for *Miss World* and just had to show me up. I felt sorry for her for not having bigger life goals than making ~~stupid~~ jello eyeballs ~~that kids go crazy over~~.

Just because Ms. Aforementioned Show-off Neighbor bedazzled her house with glitter and lights and lined her walkway with pumpkins carved into recognizable celebrities doesn't mean it's a good idea! Decorating your house for Halloween is a total waste of time. Carving a pumpkin takes—like—half the day! One year I carved one, removed and washed the pumpkin seeds, then dried and roasted them. I had to take an entire day off from work! No way could I do that every year. I needed something easier, so I bought a package of fake cobwebs at the Dollar Store. Fun fact—that ~~mother f#$%ing~~ overpriced stretchy gauze crap should come with an interior decorator because you can't "just stretch it across your front door for instant fun" like it says on the front of the bag!

After all my sweaty efforts, I was totally insulted when a judgmental trick-or-treater said, "You're supposed to take it out of the package and then stretch it to look like a spider web." Pfft. Respect your elders for once in your pampered, entitled life, Little Ms. Hannah Montana. Honestly. Then she held out her bag for some candy, and when I handed her a can of mushroom soup, she whined, "My mom says you're not allowed to give cans for treats. I'm telling!" Boo hoo! What ~~the @#$~~ is wrong with kids these days??

Kids used to appreciate stuff—when my Grade 3 teacher gave me a pretty cellophane bag filled with my favorite treats on Halloween, it was literally the second happiest day of my life (Winning *Miss Nackawic 1981* was the happiest, remember??). I vowed to do that for trick-or-treaters one day, but I didn't know you had to buy the cellophane bags and fill them yourself!! I tried it one year, but gave up after ten minutes. Did you know it takes approximately one whole minute to fill those things? Then you have to put fancy string on it because green garbage bag twist ties look super lame. I ended up just giving the trick-or-treaters one candy kiss each because I wasn't about to give away my faves—chocolate bars and chips. The little brats don't appreciate anything anyway.

Even though I enjoy the hoopla and endless giving, my favorite part of Halloween was after our boys went to bed. They 'hid' their bags of loot from me for whatever weird reason, but I always found them. Ha! Ha! Hint: The trunk of the car is a pretty obvious spot, guys. Duh. Then just like the good ol' days I gorged on Kit Kats (and Cheetos and caramels and suckers) and missed the signs that I'd gone too far—projectile vomiting, volcanic diarrhea and the dreaded ambulance ride. Live and ~~never~~ learn.

Oh, sure I wish I were a TV mom, and that I ~~gave a crap about Halloween~~ had more time on my hands, but I have to prioritize. Last time I checked, raising perfect kids and preparing for the world stage takes more than fifteen minutes/day. Frig. I'll leave Halloween to the TV moms and neighborhood ~~show-offs~~ moms with nothing else to do besides wishing they were beauty queen contenders. Jealous much? Boom.

Thanksgiving Was Super Hot, You Guys!

Thanksgiving means entertaining—my personal ~~hell~~ specialty. Woot! My quest for the perfect Thanksgiving meal always began weeks before the big day. I'd spend hours on the Interweb thingy researching stuff like: *How to cook a turkey so no one dies of salmonella poisoning.* Then I'd purchase the little extras to make the day extra special, such as pretty napkins, pilgrim hats, and a case of ~~Cabernet Sauvignon~~ cranberry sauce. Finally, I'd buy an environmentally friendly, politically correct, sustainable, non-toxic, free-range, organic, gluten-free, waterproof turkey at the local market. When the sweet farmer told me the price I'd double ~~over and scream, "WTF!!"~~ check to make sure it will feed eight people. There was never any doubt everything was going to be ~~disastrous~~ amazing!

On the morning of the big feast, I got up early and gave a silent prayer of thanks—I felt ~~defeated already~~ blessed!! I took the turkey from the fridge and rubbed it with a blend of sage, rosemary and thyme only to realize the bird was upside down! WTF. Oh, pardon me. You've never once confused a turkey's gut with its glutes, have you?! Well, aren't you just a wizard in the kitchen?! I bow to you, Oh Perfect One.

Once the bird was flipped, reherbed and ~~punched~~ salted, I slid it into the oven and quietly counted my ~~wine bottles~~ blessings to remind myself of the whole purpose of Thanksgiving—a beautiful meal with my loving family and airbrushed photos of our gathering to post on Facebook. Duh. I could hardly wait to baste the bird because it's super fun pretending I'm Martha Stewart and squirting juice from my turkey baster, except I wear goggles because of the spray that goes everywhere. I'm sure everyone wears goggles when turkey-basting.

Apparently, I also needed a hazmat suit because when I yanked (Oh really? You gently tug rather than yank do you? No one cares!) on the oven rack in my excitement, the turkey, juices, and pan tumbled into the oven and created a spontaneous bonfire. I don't remember anything after that.

My quick-thinking husband found me semi-conscious on the floor and raced into action by pouring baking soda all over the fire like he does when we play *Rescue Me, Big Boy, I'm on Fire!* When I came to, Phil was down on one knee with his head in the oven. He looked at me sideways and totally popped the question I'd been waiting to hear for twenty-five years, "Should we order in tonight?"

I screamed, "Yes!! OMG! Yes of course!! This is the happiest day of my life!! I love you!" There wasn't a dry eye in the house. Jealous much?

As the last flame was snuffed out, our extended family arrived! Don't say I said so, but I found them super dramatic, with all their hacking and crawling on all fours just because the kitchen was "filled with smoke." Cripes almighty—how many times can you hear *Stop! Drop and Roll!* before it loses its meaning? Sign up for the local drama club, why don't you? Honestly.

We ended up eating the 40-pound blackened bird because my husband's romantic suggestion that we order in didn't happen. Apparently, restaurant owners are lazy sloths and don't open on civic holidays. Whatever. We made the best of it and toasted our good health, our loving families, and the fact that the smoke damage gave me a reason to finally update the hideous paint colour of our kitchen walls to Benjamin Moore's *Silver Lining 2119-60.*

I won't pretend looking at Facebook later that night didn't hurt. Everyone was gathered around a golden turkey with all the fixins', and no one in the pictures had black lung or second-degree burns. Whatever. Each family is different and I proudly uploaded photos of our unique and special day with uplifting ~~lies~~ comments:

We went with smoked turkey this year and it was absolutely fabulous!! Inbox me for the recipe. Blessings to you and yours. xo

We were blessed to be together for a fun-filled afternoon of family games!! This one is called Silence the Smoke Detector. So many laughs!!!!

Phil popped the question again, everyone!! Yep. We're renewing our ~~house insurance~~ vows!! I am totally blessed!!!!!

After posting the seventeenth photo, it almost felt like I was seeking external validation. As I counted the 'likes' and read the ~~stupid~~ comments: *That turkey looks like it's had better days!! Ha ha!!*; *OMG, is everyone okay???* I realized something: My ~~cooking~~ photos suuuccccked. Pfft. I decided then and there that next Thanksgiving I would be ordering in, and the only pictures I'd be posting on Facebook would be ones of my family gathered around a perfect meal. I'll be the one wearing the *Miss World 2018* sash obviously.

@Miss Nackawic1981 #bah #humbug

Christmas is super hard—the shopping, wrapping, decorating and baking ~~hash brownies~~ make it impossible to keep my ~~AA promise~~ head on straight! As if that weren't enough, I always felt I had to send out Christmas cards filled with ~~lies~~ my family's accomplishments and airbrushed photos of me. When our boys were young and I had energy, I totally loved sending cards to friends and family—I wanted our holiday greetings to be perfect, so I pulled out all ~~my hair~~ the stops. One year I decided to seal my ~~hand-painted~~ cards with wax like Martha ~~@#$ing~~ Stewart does. Because I don't have one hundred assistants like Ms. Aforementioned Decorating Diva, I spilled it by mistake, slipped in the hot wax, and then burnt my tongue when I tasted it because I thought it smelt like cranberries. Sue me. After the first responders left, I decided to scale things down a bit and the cards were the first thing to go.

Cards. Schmards. Last year I turned to Twitter instead. I tweeted my hopes, wishes and ~~cries for help~~ updates for the holidays. Boom. The time I'd usually spent licking ~~wine bottles~~ envelopes would free me up for the other parts of the holidays I adore—fending off Santa at the mall (handsy little bugger—Ha! Ha!), plunging into ~~debt~~ the colourful wrapping paper, and spending lots of time ~~alone in the kitchen~~ with my precious family. On top of all that, at this time of year I also had to update my *Miss World* vision board and take my annual Christmas bikini—red with white fur obviously—photo for my portfolio. There were only so many hours in a day—something had to give.

So I told my friends if they followed me on Twitter, they'd hear from me at all hours of the day!! If that weren't exciting enough, I even offered the first one hundred followers a photo of me the night I won *Miss Nackawic 1981*.

@MissNackawic1981 *2016-12-07* Christmas is gonna be awesome, you guys! I love the holidays so hard. Sending love your way xo #feliznavidad

@MissNackawic1981 *2016-12-08* Listening to Celine Dion sing Silent Night while I make meat pies. Super poignant! Wish I could sing like that. Kidding! I can!! #obviously

@MissNackawic1981 *2016-12-09* Malls r super busy! Line-ups to see Miss Nackawic 1981-er-Santa. Too cute! #soft #tweet

@MissNackawic1981 *2016-12-10* Putting up the tree tonight! #awesome #family #tradition

@MissNackawic1981 *2016-12-10* Going through tree ornaments and found adorable macaroni snowflakes the boys made in kindergarten. #they #used #to #care #hmmmph

@MissNackawic1981 *2016-12-10* Tree crooked. Hubby blaming me for not holding it straight. Grumpypants #LOL

@MissNackawic1981 *2016-12-10* On the first day of Christmas my teen boys gave to me: Blank looks as I decorate the tree. Alone. #whatever #Pfft

@MissNackawic1981 *2016-12-11* Looks like snow globe outside! Took me-er-Phil 45 minutes to clean off car. Pretty but annoying #winter #is #super #hard

@MissNackawic1981 *2016-12-12* Asked my boys what they wanted for Christmas. They said: Donmzarmfgr #huh? #enunciate #4 #once

@MissNackawic1981 *2016-12-13* Just spent 2 hours and $500 at grocery store. And forgot milk #WTF

@MissNackawic1981 *2016-12-15* Mmmmm. Baileys is so delish in my coffee. And smoothies. And cereal. And mashed potatoes #judge #yourself #Miss #Sobriety

@MissNackawic1981 *2016-12-17* Dear Driver of 2013 Black Prius, Licence Plate L214Y who cut me off in mall parking lot: I'll gut you like a pig if I see you again. #sonofab#$

@MissNackawic1981 *2016-12-19* Mmmmm. Sleeping pills and vodka #judge #yourself #Miss #Sobriety

@MissNackawic1981 *2016-12-20* Mmmmm. Shortbread cookies are delish. I made 36 and I ate 18. Maternity pants r tight #not #pregnant

@MissNackawic1981 *2016-12-21* Witnessed death by trampling at Sobeys in the frozen turkey section. No time to report it—too much to do! #judge #yourself #Miss #Morality

@MissNackawic1981 *2016-12-22* Mmmmmm...Lighter fluid. Tree on fire! #oops *#911*

@MissNackawic1981 *2016-12-23* Fourth trip to mall. Not wearing tiara this time—too much commotion. #need #bodyguard #obviously

@MissNackawic1981 *2016-12-24* Ran out of wrapping paper. Back to the #$%ing mall. Regret taking hostage. #Hindsight #20/20

@MissNackawic1981 *2016-12-25* Merry Christmas to all my friends and family. I love you all and I hope you have a wonderful holiday. Also I ho

@MissNackawic1981 *2016-12-25* Stupid #$%ing 140-character rule! Also I hope you don't outdo me on Facebook! #don't #overpost

@MissNackawic1981 *2016-12-25* If you unfollowed me (I used to have 24 followers and since the holidays I'm down to 18. WTF!!), you're not getting that autographed photo of Miss Nackawic 1981 and furthermore I'm taking you off my Christmas card list even though I'm never sending ano

@MissNackawic1981 *2016-12-25* another #$%ing Christmas card as long as I live because next year I'll be in the Bermuda Triangle on Dec 25 relaxing for a change!! #u #heard #me #peace #out #Pfft

Boxing Day Totally ~~Sucks~~ Rocks!

Christmas was super ~~hard~~ awesome, but I totally ~~sucked at~~ rocked Boxing Day. I loved so much about it—making turkey soup, ~~igniting~~ pitching the tree outside, putting away the decorations, hanging ~~up on VISA representatives for inappropriate badgering~~ out with my awesome family, and mainlining ~~vodka~~ coffee while in my PJs. Boom. And it's so much fun to return the gifts that didn't make the cut on Christmas morning.

Just because the entire galaxy flocks to the mall on Boxing Day ~~does~~ doesn't mean it's a bad idea. Replacing that medium-sized midnight-blue T-shirt with a large baby-blue T-shirt felt like life or death. I put on my tiara and my big girl panties and found the courage most people lack—I'm not only breathtaking, I'm super brave.

Crowds. Schmowds. Pfft. I found a parking space in thirty-seven minutes flat. I suppose if you had a ~~homemade~~ *Miss Nackawic 1981* parking pass in your windshield, you'd get breaks like that too. Too bad I'm the only one who has that! Once inside the mall, I blurted, *Miss Nackawic 1981 is in the houussee!!* Obviously everyone was deaf or had Alzheimer's because I saw nothing but vacant looks. Honestly. You'd think the tiara would be a dead giveaway. Whatever.

It's no secret I'm patient—Duh, look how long I'm willing to wait for my dream to come true—but the everyday irritations can get under my sash. After waiting in line for hours without even so much as an autograph request, I considered taking ~~a hostage~~ off. Then I saw the woman in front of me actually give full-blown birth to twin boys, and I got some much-needed perspective. If she could wait that long, then so could I. Plus, how was that poor woman going to return her stuff now that it was covered in placenta?? Gross. I suddenly felt blessed.

The line was moving slower than my ~~mother #$%ing~~ Miss World dream, but the upside was getting to see those adorable twins grow up! They had changed so much since they were born in the doorway of Old Navy—Garrett could sit up by himself, but Dakota was content to just roll on the mall floor. Cuties. I felt honored when Diane (their mother, obviously) asked me to be their godmother, but I had to say no because of potential pageant-related gigs. Just as I was adjusting to life as a hard core mall-dweller, I heard, "I can help the next person in line." I felt a little guilty for taking Diane's place, but it was hardly my fault she had to leave the line to chase her boys. We all make choices in life.

I walked up to the cash register, removed the T-shirt from the bag and said, "I'd like this in another size and colour please." The cat-eyed, pouty-lipped sales associate with the nametag *Sofeeya* began clicking and clacking on the keyboard. After fifteen minutes of this, I calmly asked, "Are you hiding behind that keyboard because you're too shy to ask for my autograph? Is that what this is about?" She pretended she didn't hear me. Classic jealousy. She came up for air just as I heard Garrett's first word—he scurried over, pointed at me and uttered, "Queen". Ha! Ha! Too cute! We didn't practice it that way but *Miss Nackawic* is tricky even for me to say! He'll get it.

Finally, Sofeeya finished clacking on her keyboard and came 'this close' to looking at me when she said, "I just have a few questions before I can release the new T-shirt." I adore getting-to-know-you games, so I was all in. She started with the basics: "Name? Street? Postal code? Phone number? Reason for returning the merchandise? Allergies? Eye color? Hobbies? Favorite food? Deepest secret? Biggest regret?" Wow—I hadn't told anyone about the time I stole that satin hat from Sears when I was ~~eighteen~~ twelve, but I did feel better once it was out. I was really starting to feel a connection with Sofeeya—she knew me inside and out, after all!!

Next, she scanned the T-shirt, clacked on the keyboard for the rest of the afternoon, and then spoke into the James Bond-esque microphone that was pinned to her strappy camisole, "~~Code Blue~~. Exchange at front desk please. Exchange at front desk. I repeat: Exchange at front desk." The employee standing directly beside her spoke into his mic next, "I'm on it." He fetched the new T-shirt while I asked Sofeeya to send me a Facebook friend request. She did her whole *I'm deaf* thing again, but I wondered if she was just an insecure ~~weirdo~~ introvert, so I didn't push it.

Her colleague returned with the T-shirt and Sofeeya scanned it and slipped it into the bag. I tried to make eye contact with her while I waited for the printer to spit out a lengthy receipt that needed to be signed in seventeen different places, but she was hell-bent on ignoring me and rolling her eyes. Fine. Be that way. I grabbed my bag, tripped over Dakota, and headed for the door. I heard Sofeeya yell, "Wait!" Boom.

"Want my Twitter handle?" I asked. She rudely ignored me once again and said, "You have to fill out our survey, write your name on a ballot to win a pair of jeans, answer a skill-testing question, and provide ~~a urine sample~~ us with your email address." Well, finally we were getting somewhere! She was begging for my email address—talk about playing hard to get!

Lesson learned—don't ~~go to the mall on Boxing Day~~ get too close to store employees or people in long line-ups. Sure, it's a dopamine hit when you make a new friend, but then you have to learn to live without them. I often wonder how Garrett and Dakota turned out, and, more importantly, why in God's name Sofeeya reported me to the Facebook police. Since when is making hourly friend requests a crime?? OMG. Maybe this whole thing happened so I'd be forced to take a deeper look at myself and my potential insecurities. Nah—that doesn't make sense. I'm ~~delusional~~ perfect just the way I am—the only thing I might have to work on is not being so vulnerable and giving, but that's hardly a character flaw. As if.

Section 2

Life with Boys Is Super ~~Confusing~~ Awesome

Rules for Raising Boys

Once my sweet boys became teenagers, they mumbled a lot and refused to look at me, but they were still able to do some amazing and selfless things like inhaling a refrigerator while blindfolded and asleep, walking through blizzards wearing only a polyester hoodie, and breathing. Once our brilliant angels mastered those super hard things, I did something terrible—I asked them to help around the house. I regret springing it on them because it caused a lot of ~~police visits~~ confusion and bad feelings.

I took it upon my awesome self to create some ~~useless~~ advice for moms out there who might be ~~mainlining~~ struggling with getting their teens to help with household chores. You're totally welcome.

☺ **Start when they're young**–Toddlers are adorable, but also lazy. If they can push those ~~stupid~~ toy lawnmowers around your house, they can push a vacuum cleaner or broom.

☺ **Start with the basics**–Give your sons a tour of the kitchen and say things like, "~~You do SFA around here!!~~ This is an oven. This is a dishwasher." Show them the buttons and have them practise opening and closing appliances. They love pushing ~~my~~ buttons! Precious little fellas.

☺ **Use a calm and firm but loving tone**–Speak softly. If you raise your voice, they might get offended and ignore you, and you don't want that. Say nice things like, "Even though Mommy is asking you to put your clothes in the hamper rather than beside the ~~mother #$%ing~~ hamper, it doesn't mean Mommy doesn't love you, sweetie—it just means Mommy will have to go away to that special hospital again because she's exhausted and has nothing left for the pageant. And Mommy needs the pageant."

☺ **Use consequences**–~~Always~~ Sometimes they will ignore your requests. Give them consequences like withholding hugs and eye contact. They totally ~~love~~ hate that!

☺ **Be clear**–When you talk to your teenagers, be sure to have their full attention even if it means ~~smashing their iPhones to smithereens with a hammer~~, waiting for a few ~~hours~~ minutes. Also enunciate so they understand your big words: Please hang ~~me~~ your ja-ck-et in the clo-set.

🐝 **Set realistic expectations**–Don't ask them to do ~~two~~ a million things! It will only upset your sweet angels. Be reasonable. Asking them to turn off a light AND lift their feet so you can wipe the table underneath them will literally force them to turn ~~up the volume on the TV~~ away from you. Use your head.

🐝 **Be super patient**–When you ask your strapping, athletic sons to perform a challenging task such as taking out the garbage, they might mumble, "mmbjjifazz." Their eyes might look dead, and they could even slur their speech. It's super scary because it looks like a stroke, but you can test for that. Just put a few strips of bacon in the microwave. If they shuffle toward the smell, you will know they are healthy and fine. Then take out the garbage yourself.

To be the best mom ever, you must choose your battles and monitor your ~~pill intake~~ expectations. Teenage boys—bless their precious hearts—show their love by sleeping, eating, and driving your car to cool places with their friends. If you're still filled with white hot rage because they don't help around the house, you could always teach them to fold towels into cool origami animals ~~around their necks~~ to make it fun for them! Ooooh.... origami towel creations could be my talent in the upcoming pageant!! Boom.

Sandwich Shapes Matter. Obviously

Get this—our firstborn baby boy, Alex, got accepted into medical school after only three years of university, and it's all because of me!! EEEEE!!! You heard me. Well...maybe not **all** because of me, but I obviously take most of the credit. Try reading a few studies for once, and you'll see that to create future doctors, you must be a ~~neurotic~~ nurturing mother, ~~pretend to~~ participate in their interests, and make super outstanding school lunches. I did all of that and then some. Boom.

When my sweet boys were in their early elementary years, I was literally ~~certifiable~~ obsessed with making their lunches—I totally wanted them and the world to know I loved them to the moon and back. Don't be jealous, but, when the other moms called me *Hover Mother*, I shivered with pride.

Every night, I would make my boys' sandwiches and then cut them into shapes that would make them smile—hearts, circles, tetrahedrons—you name it. I shudder to think of where they would have ended up if they'd had to settle for triangle-shaped sandwiches. Good Lord, what some kids go through! To top off the awesome sandwiches I made, I would then slip a note into their lunch bags. Gosh, I can barely remember what they said, but here's the gist: *Have a good day! See you after school! You will become a doctor one day ~~or I will withhold my love~~!* Boom.

Speaking of math, shortly after the sandwich/note phase, I noticed that ~~I was gradually being phased out~~ our boys were pulling away from me. They began to take a keen interest in math and science, which I totally hated!! All of a sudden, I didn't understand what ~~the #$%~~ they were talking about! I majored in English, and I envisioned us reciting poetry together, not multiplication tables! WTF. I totally freaked out when they turned from me—their giver of life—and I insisted they recite Shakespeare every night. I still get goosebumps when I remember those precious preschoolers mumbling: *This above all else: To thine own sewlf be twue.* Swoon.

Spoiler alert—despite my poetry demands, Alex and Max continued to conduct stupid science experiments, understood that *pi* didn't come with meringue, and get this—one of them even had the nerve to correctly use the words 'string theory' in a sentence in Grade 5. It's not like I didn't understand any of it. Obviously I ~~failed~~ took high school science and math courses, so I totally understood stuff like a polynomial is a shape with nine equal sides. When they threw out words like *parabolas, kwantum* fisix (Oh really?? Well, how do **you** spell it, Captain Intelligence?) and the *Periodic Table*, I tried to fit in by saying ~~wrong and inappropriate~~ things like: *Oh! I know what **that** is!! Back in the day, I used the Periodic Table to chart my menstrual cycles and I'm here to tell you it's a total crock and does NOT—I repeat—NOT work! **You** try counting 14 days from Fe (Iron) and see how many times you get pregnant. The 'Idiotic Table' might be a better name for it!*

Whatever. I'm over it. Even though I don't speak their language, I do other awesome and helpful things around here! Fun facts: I make a mean ~~martini~~ shepherd's pie, I can grocery shop in under thirteen minutes (Jealous much?), and I can pull together a dumpster with the perfect, well placed throw cushion. Boom. The moral of this story is you need to cut your kids' sandwiches into super awesome shapes, smother them with love and kisses ~~and SPF 90 sunscreen~~, and maybe—just maybe—one day you too will have brilliant kids...even if you don't always understand what they're talking about and they outright refuse to recite poetry with you. Pfft.

Four Letter Word

The month of September used to make me wish I were ~~dead~~ a TV mom because they always show off and buy school supplies *before* the first day of school. Whatever. I always found it hard to shop for clothes and school supplies and then fill out millions of school forms when I already had so much pageant stuff on my plate!! ARGH. Declaring ~~bankruptcy~~ schedules and bed times for the boys was stressful too, and I honestly found it hard to stay ~~sober~~ sane! But the absolute worst part of September was the four letter word that often lead to family ~~court~~ tension—*lunches*. Do you have to count *every single* letter?! Who cares if there are seven letters?! Focus!

When our sweet boys started kindergarten I took ~~little yellow pills~~ great pleasure in making their lunches. Each evening I would lovingly wash fruit, and make tiny hand-painted piñatas filled with homemade gluten-free, organic granola. (as all amazing moms do…) Then I would make their sandwiches. Average moms make average triangle-shaped sandwiches, but I was far from ~~sane~~ average. I cut them into hearts, squares, octagons, hexagons and prisms obviously. Unfortunately, it totally backfired. My creative shapes singlehandedly sparked their interest in math and science and before long they were using big fancy words I couldn't understand! Sometimes it just doesn't pay to be a perfect mother who is the envy of all.

So over the years, I lost my will to ~~live~~ make lunches. It was hard to keep lunch-related food in the house because our growing boys ate everything that wasn't nailed down and even some stuff that *was*—like the floorboards. I had to hide lunch snacks in the goofiest places like the dishwasher, the chimney, and ~~my mouth~~ the car manifold, but they always found them! By the end of the week, there was nothing left for those ~~mother @#$ing~~ lunches, so they had to settle for whatever I could find—uncooked rice, croutons, and ~~staplers~~ lettuce sandwiches…without the bread. Phil was no help. His contribution had always been to draw a picture of tractors on the boys' napkins to make them smile. I noticed his pictures were becoming disturbing—once he drew a picture in black crayon of himself being flattened by a steamroller. Thanks for helping. ~~Idiot.~~

I needed to ~~be *Miss World*~~ find a solution once and for all. Making lunches totally consumed me, and I couldn't help but wonder if I'd catered to them too much... *This one* didn't want ham. *That one* wanted fresh Alaskan snow crab and beef tenderloin with a side of foie gras. Nah...all kids ate that stuff. I was doing everything right, obviously.

At the end of every school day, my first question wasn't, "How was your day?" or "Did you ~~get beat up again~~ do your best?" but rather, "Did you eat that f#$%ing lunch I slaved over because, so help me God, if you shared one morsel of it with a hungry child—or worse—left a mayonnaise-laced sandwich to rot in your lunch box, I will literally swallow this entire bottle of pills right now!" Things always went super quiet after that because the pills kicked in.

When I came to, I'd usually call a family meeting. If no one showed up, I'd simply change the venue to the TV room where they were sprawled out in front of the screen. They became super ~~dis~~engaged when I started to speak, "Hey guys. Listen up! I know you're used to me making your lunches, and I do an awesome job of it, but I'm totally exhausted, and I need some help around here okay?" The tension was thick. Finally someone spoke. "We can't hear the TV!" The meeting was a total ~~bust~~ success! I decided to throw ~~myself down the stairs~~ together their lunch for the next day and for old times' sake, I included a little note:

I hope you enjoy your tetrahedron-shaped lobster sandwich and sweet potato medallions and that you will become a doctor one day. Did you read the Power Point presentation I sent you with the highlights of the family meeting ~~since you weren't paying attention~~? If you refer to Section B Subsection 1A, you will note that Mommy is hormonal these days. Google it. Sometimes I threaten things, and then I simmer down and change my mind. I will make your lunches until you are a big man, sweetie, but could you put your dishes in the dishwasher? That would be super awesome!! Also, I'm sorry if I scared you, but I literally only took half that bottle of pills. I would never take a whole bottle!
PS Sorry this note took 3 napkins. Ha! Ha!

PPS I'm thinking of bacon wrapped scallops with a side of garlic mashed potatoes for your lunch next week. Thoughts? Mommy loves you. xo
PPPS Do your friends know Mommy is Miss Nackawic 1981? It's not a secret so you can tell them.

H-E- Double Hockey Sticks

Hockey games in Nackawic were super fun, and my friends and I were always there in the stands cheering! When our high school team scored a goal, to show our support we would lift our shirts and scream, "Two! Four! Six! Eight! Who do we appreciate? Nackawic!! Nackawic!! Hit the losers with your stick!!" and polish up our brass knuckles for the post-game parking lot brawl. Apparently, they do it differently in big fancy cities like Moncton. I wish someone had warned me before our boys signed up for the ~~dumb~~ sport.

When our precious boys signed up for hockey, I had no idea what I was in for. Get this—some of the games were during supper hour (WTF!); the games weren't televised, so I had to actually go to the freezing cold rinks; and because the other ~~idiot~~ hockey moms were so into the games, I had to pretend I was interested too instead of signing autographs at the rink!! All they wanted to talk about was hockey. It was super hard to bond with them because their priorities were messed up but I had to try.

For the first game, I kept it simple and just let my awesome personality ~~disorder~~ shine through with my subtle observations:

OMG. I just love our team's costumes!

Woot!! We scored!! Check out my boobies, everybody!!

Hey, ref!! Your ~~#$%ing mother smokes crack~~ glasses must be fogged up!

I sat alone for most of that ~~season~~ game. Pfft. I didn't want to sit with them anyway.

Even though I was asked to sit three bleachers behind the other un-friendly, weird hockey moms, I could still hear them. They seemed super informed, so I eavesdropped big time. Suckas! I'd soon be the queen of hockey moms if I just listened carefully. Also I'd impress my family with my new hockey know-how. After the game, I literally killed it during our family's post-hockey chat at home:

Me: Hey, guys! What a game!! The reffing totally sucked, eh?

Phil: Not really, no.

Me: Oh... Josh's mom said it did though...

Crickets. . .

Alex: Hey, Dad. Did you see my breakaway?

Me: Ooooh! I saw it!! Ask me!! Wait. What's a breakaway?

Crickets. . .

Me: Sam's mom said ~~she's taken a lover~~ his penalty was totally ridiculous!! He was on his way to the bench when the ref called 'too many men'— wasn't his fault and he shouldn't have got two minutes for that!! Dumb call, right?

Max: (Rolls eyes) Gawd, Mom. We don't even have a Sam on our team...

Me: I knew that. I meant Zach. Whatever. It doesn't matter who it happened to because there can never be 'too many men' on or off the ice so there! Stupidest rule I ever heard of. Hmmmph.

Obviously the loser hockey moms on our team hadn't read the rule book, either! Fine. I would just learn this ~~stupid~~ game on my own by paying attention during the game instead of uploading selfies on Facebook. It worked! In no time flat, I could tell an *offside* from *icing*; I could figure out if I was in the right rink, and I could tell which kid on the ice was mine by yelling, "Sweetie!! If you're on the ice right now, please look up at Mommy and scratch your nose! I forget your number but I love you to the moon and back!"

Just as I was becoming an amazing hockey mom, something terrible happened! Max decided to ~~finish me off~~ become a goalie! My therapist says that was the root of a lot of my hostility, but what does ~~that #$%ing idiot~~ she know, anyway!??

I hated that every goal my boy didn't stop would reflect horribly on me. Plus, I had to learn a different set of rules for goalies! If an opponent scored on my baby, I'd yell, "~~Stop letting goals in for crissakes! The parents already hate me!~~ It was a *power play*, sweetie! Not your fault. I still love you to the moon and back!" Then I'd take ~~fourteen~~ large swigs from my bottle of *Fire-*

ball, as all goalie moms do. Another trick I learned—when there's a delayed penalty, don't scream, "I don't care what that miserable ~~piece of @#$%~~ coach says, you get back in that net! You didn't do anything wrong, my precious little man!!" Everyone turned to stare at me…in silent solidarity obviously.

Guess what?! After attending nine million games that season, I learned practically ~~nothing~~ everything there was to know about hockey! I could even *predict* the penalties! You heard me. Take for example the time I was selling 50/50 tickets during one of Alex's games. I had just stuffed a $20 bill into my bra for a $5 ticket (Oh yea?? **Prove** I didn't give him his change back, Ms. Private Investigator!), when, out of the corner of my eye, I saw my firstborn baby boy careening toward the boards to get the puck just like I taught him. Then I saw a brute with zero brain activity, going after my child with super scary speed. I said to myself, "Pretty sure there's going to be a *boarding* call here, and my child is going to be ~~a paraplegic~~ needing his momma."

When I saw him get hit from behind, drop to the ice, and not resurface, I obviously did what any caring and knowledgeable hockey mom would do. I ripped the rink door off the hinges with my pinkie, and beat ~~the crap out of the criminal who did this~~ a path to my barely conscious child who was surrounded by his coach, father, and teammates. I put my face two centimetres from his and freaked out, "OMG! Are you okay??? Try to focus, sweetie… on me—not your father. I'm the one who pushed you out of a tiny opening in my body after fourteen hours of labour without so much as a Gravol!"

My husband obviously felt threatened because right after I asked our son, "Can you wiggle your toes?? How many fingers am I holding up? Who's your favorite parent?" he hissed, "*Get. Off. The. Ice.*" I don't know why he had to enunciate so dramatically. It's not like I was deaf. ~~Idiot.~~

After several years of sitting on cold benches, I decided I was too ~~stupid~~ tired to learn any more hockey rules. Since the boys refused to quit hockey like I asked them to, I decided to just blend into the background and quietly support them by lifting my shirt every time I heard a whistle. It worked in Nackawic.

Please Help Me! My Son is Having a Stroke!!!

For your information, our boys certainly *did* speak in full sentences once upon a time, and I have the footage to prove it! In fact, at the end of each day when they were preschoolers, we had a nightly ritual called *Talk Time* where my husband and I would sit on the edge of their beds while the boys rambled on about their days—*We had a supply teacher, my sandwich was on brown bread so I threw it out (WTF!!), we learned a new song, I drew a picture for you, Josh wouldn't take turns on the swing. (WTF! I'll make that kid pay if it's the last thing I do...)* They didn't mumble, shrug their shoulders or pretend they ~~didn't know me~~ were deaf, not that those things bother me in the least. Pfft. Hardly even notice.

As they got older, their stories became super short without any eye contact or ~~words~~ details. Then they became teenagers. One evening, something terrible happened that haunts me to this day. I had asked Max to dry the dishes after supper. He looked around the house like he didn't know where the dishes were. He was totally confused. When I asked him a second time, he said, "wazzadeshwe?" and walked away, knocking over a carton of milk by mistake. Then he was too confused to clean it up!! OMG! I had seen the commercials, and I knew the signs—lack of eye contact, confusion and garbled speech. I called 911 immediately!

Operator: What is your emergency?

Me: Please help me!! Dear God, my son is having a full blown actual stroke! I can't understand a word he's saying, and he is super confused and uncoordinated!

Operator: How old is your son, ma'am?

Me: Fifteen...but I didn't call you to chit chat for crissakes!! Do you want to know his hobbies too?? Hair color??? Do your job and help me save my son!!

Operator: Calm down, ma'am. Your son isn't having a stroke, but, by the sounds of things, ~~you might be~~ he's experiencing normal teen withdrawal. He'll eventually grow ~~up and leave you forever~~ out of it.

Me: I knew that...

Frig. A stroke would have been a better explanation than my loinfruit actually *choosing* not to talk to his life source! Whatever. Fine then. If the days of talking in full sentences were over, I would hit below the belt and buy our boys cell phones so we could communicate in a new way. Since talking was so *yesterday*, they'd just have to bare their souls to me through texting. Boom. Solved.

The boys learnt how super ~~neurotic~~ cool and hip I was when I totally embraced their world. Don't be jealous as you read the intimate conversations I had via texts with my grown embryos:

Me: Hi sweetie☺! It's me, mom. Does my name show up on your phone thingy or will I have to tell you it's me every time, which is super annoying so I really hope not. LOLA!!!!! I ho

Me: Shoot! Sorry!!! I pushed the big button by mistake and my text sent before I was finished. LOLA!!!!! I hope you are having a good day. I love you to the moon and back! Bye for now!! ☺☺☺☺

Crickets. . .

Me: Hellooooooo?? My phone doesn't work! ☹☹☹☹ I sent you a text five minutes ago and you didn't respond. Did you get my text??

Grown Embryo: yep

Stupid me!! I sent that text during school hours when they were busy. Duh. Next time, I made sure to send it outside of school hours.

Me: Hey! What's up? You may have noticed I'm not home. I'm at the grocery store as always. LOLA!!!

Crickets. . .

Me: Hello?? Are you home???

Grown embryo: yep

Finally, I saw a pattern. I had to ask a question!!! Duh. This was super hard to figure out!

Me: Hi pumpkin. How was your day?

Grown embryo: Good

BINGO!!!!

Me: I had a good day too, sweet man.

Crickets. . .

Me: jirs ig jinwqrll?

Grown embryo: ????

Me: Oooopppss!! I couldn't find my glasses!! LOLA. I meant—Lots of
homework?

Grown embryo: what's LOLA???

Me: It means to laugh a lot, sweetie! What ~~does your voice sound like? Has
it changed yet? Did you draw me a picture today~~? are you up to?

Grown embryo: OMG it's LOL, not LOLA, mom. Wow.

Such fun!!! I was totally hooked! Every time I heard my phone buzz with
a text from the boys unloading their emotions on me, the dopamine rush
was unreal! And for your information, I ~~do~~ don't need ~~words~~ full sentences,
facial expressions, and eye contact to know what's going on my kids' lives,
thank you very much. Trust me, I'd have known if ~~Josh wasn't taking turns
on the swings~~ something was wrong. It's important to go with the flow
when parenting—I know I make it look easy. I wish getting information on
the upcoming *Miss World* pageant were as easy. Why so secretive??? OMG.

Friggin' Home Wreckers!

Every morning, it was always the same thing. I'd come downstairs, see this and call 911:

Me: Help!! My home has been ransacked!

911 Operator: Is that you again, Colleen? Sigh. Do we have to go through this every morning?? There's nothing we can do! It's your family!

Then I'd remember. It was worse than being robbed—I lived with three males. I'd scoop the cushions and punch ~~the wall~~ them to make them super fluffy again, prop them on the couch, and pull out my trusty ruler to make sure they were totally symmetrical...as all ~~freaks~~ decorator mom types do. After the cushions were refluffed, I'd take a ~~muscle relaxant~~ deep breath and relax, knowing everyone was asleep and not wrecking my friggin' house! I can only pray my *Miss World* accommodations have untouched throw cushions. I deserve at least that.

All I ever wanted was to be an awesome beauty queen with a pretty home that made people super jealous. Instead, I got a loving family and the ~~trashed~~ lived-in look. Just my luck! I don't get it. On sitcoms, throw pillows are never on the floor! No one in my household understood the importance of a fab home and worse—they touched things that should never be moved, much less manhandled. OMG. They thought throw blankets were for warmth on a cold winter's night, that the hand-carved birch chess board on the coffee table was for recreational purposes, and get this—that it was okay to push the decorative cushions aside when they sat on the couch. Sometimes, I wondered why I even bothered ~~living~~ trying!

I tried using my ~~passive aggressive~~ sweet, patient voice:

Hey guys, would you mind not using that white cushion as a placemat for your blood-red spaghetti which is literally a disaster waiting to happen?

Honey, I'd rather you didn't lay your sweaty body on all eight throw cushions directly after your work-out.

When I got no response, I tried signs.

I wasn't getting through! They couldn't get that ~~I was having a mental breakdown~~ cushions tie everything together, add 'punch', and make the furniture pop. Honestly, it was like we were speaking different languages! It was time for another family meeting, my ~~bihourly~~ weekly attempt to "change things around here." We gathered in the family room, and I asked ~~the idiots~~ them to listen super carefully.

I pointed to the strewn and squished pillows and told them it made me feel ~~less regal~~ disorganized and devastated. I chose my words carefully and kept it basic by using terms like *cozy, feng shui* and ~~rehab~~ *accent colors*. I demonstrated the proper way to position a throw cushion, and how to preserve it by not sitting or drooling on it. The meeting went super well, and they actually asked some pretty hard-hitting questions:

What's a throw cushion?

Can you turn up the TV?

When's supper? We're starving.

After the question/answer period, I tried to get them involved in decorating, so I asked them to show me how *they* might arrange the cushions. Obviously it was time for another DNA test because here's what the home wreckers came up with. OMG. I literally give up.

Driving Miss Crazy

You may find this hard to believe but I have one flaw—I was super neurotic in the passenger seat when our boys were learning to drive. Literally, the day our firstborn, Alex, turned 16, he *just had* to get his driver's permit, regardless of how it affected *my* mental health. Everyone knows teenage boys are incapable of operating a light switch, much less a vehicle for the *lovovgod*!! The thought of my royal heir behind the wheel of a moving deadly weapon totally freaked me out, so I did what any normal parent would do: I buried the car keys in the Atlantic Ocean; I petitioned the Supreme Court to change the beginning driving age to 39; and I sprawled in the driveway behind the car screaming, "Over my totally ripped dead body!!"

It's hardly my fault I was a total wreck—the world had done it to me. For starters, I'd been used to riding on parade floats where the speed was 3 km/h and my hair stayed in place. I didn't worry about hitting a brick wall and having to redo my make-up. Not only that, my husband was ~~a maniac~~ an aggressive driver who made me super nervous. Every time I got into the car with him, I would recite ~~the Hail Mary~~ my mantra: *Keep calm. Carry on ~~without me after the crash~~.* Things always got better once the horse tranquilizers kicked in, but only until I woke up. Then I would go totally nuts:

AAAHHHHH!!! Moose! Moose!!

OMG!! I forgot my flame-retardant jumpsuit and matching helmet!!

Please make sure my tiara and sash find a good home when I'm gone!!

I wasn't always this uptight—duh…total understatement. When I got my driver's license at sixteen, I rolled ~~the car six times~~ my eyes at my freaked-out parents in the passenger seat when they made annoying and totally weird comments like:

The speed limit is 100. You're going 280!!

Stop staring at yourself in the rearview mirror!!

You just killed a rabbit and two raccoons!

It's not like I killed a *person*. Honestly. Maybe I'm super ~~insane~~ cautious because my parents freaked out so much on me—not my fault. They say to get over a fear you have to face it head-on. Um...That's exactly what I was afraid of—a HEAD-ON collision!!! White water rafting straight down Niagara Falls would be a day at the spa compared to my dread of death at 100 km/h with my ~~newborns~~ teenagers at the wheel.

I rose to the occasion though. Whenever our competent son wanted to go for a drive, I would say, "~~Ask your father.~~ I'm ~~hammered~~ in!" I simply buried my fear and let him weave through the city streets. I stayed ~~medicated~~ cool and made casual conversation to divert his attention from the ginormous hole I made in the floorboard by pressing my imaginary brake one too many ~~million~~ times.

Our son absolutely adored our windshield time—he loved to chat and said stuff like, "Mom, you seem ~~insane~~ nervous." Driving around with no distractions ~~other than me with a loudspeaker screaming out the window. Clear the road!! Go home, everyone!!~~ made for some awesome bonding. He even shared his feelings with me, "I prefer driving with Dad." It was totally amazing to spend this kind of time with him.

Get this—both of our boys ended up being a better driver than I am. Pfft. Whatever. Their driving records are super flawless, but so is mine if you don't count that one incident in the Walmart parking lot. It's not that I don't trust them—it's just that I'm a ~~control freak~~ worrier who thinks a shift in the wind will blow us off the highway and into the side of a moose standing in front of a brick wall that's on fire. I mean, who doesn't think these things?? Duh.

I may even consider hiring them to be my *Miss World* chauffeur once I win...if they keep the speed below two km/h so that my hair will stay in place which obviously matters as much as staying alive.

Black is ~~Stupid~~ the New Black

Teenage boys need their mothers like a snowstorm needs a lawnmower, not that I ~~cried myself to sleep~~ cared. Once our boys turned thirteen, they only relied on me to feed them and to be their chauffeur. Whatever. I just wanted to be their role model for at least one other thing before they left the perfect nest I made for them—graduation tux shopping. Surely, my ability to tear through a mall under harsh fluorescent lighting would impress them. I could help them through the most wonderful parts of prom shopping—crying fits, battered self-esteem, and ~~bankruptcy~~ mother-son squabbles. I could hardly wait!!!

I started shopping for my ~~Miss World~~ high school prom dress in September of Grade 3, so imagine my shock when Alex showed literally zero shopping urgency in his grad year. He ignored my hourly reminders that we should go tux shopping immediately to avoid disappointment. He just shrugged his shoulders and mumbled, "Doesntmattr mom." WTF! With prom one week away, I ~~screamed horrible things~~ gently nudged him until he finally caved.

Three days before grad prom, we finally walked into the men's clothing store. Boom. I got that warm glow that only fresh fabric can give me. And my ~~barely conscious~~ awesome and excited boy was at my side! Swoon. I couldn't wait to see my super strapping son try on at least twelve(teen) different tuxedos! As I wandered to a rack of dashing-looking suits, I heard, "Over here, Mom." He was studying a cold and sterile laminated poster filled with pictures of tuxes. Pictures?? Then he pointed, "That one."

Wait… What?? This couldn't be happening to me! He chose his tux from a poster in under three seconds! I didn't even get to say the words I've been waiting to say since he was born—"Turn around, sweetie. Button the top button. Tilt your head to the left and smile with your eyes. You're so handsome and mommy loves you to the moon and back!" It was literally starting to feel like this was all about him!

I stayed super calm and reminded myself I still had the joy of choosing cummerbund, tie, and shoes! Total awesomeness!! I held a totally chic burgundy paisley tie and asked, "Oooh! What do you think of this one?" His lips barely moved when he said these terrible words—"Nah. Black." I said, "Um, but sweetie, what color is your date's dress?" He replied, "Doesntmattr. Black goes with everything." Why did I have to do such an amazing job teaching him that black is the perfect accent??

Shoes were next…

Sales clerk: Round or square toe?

Alex: Square

   Suspenders…

Sales clerk: Black or white?

Alex: Black

With all this black, I worried he might be in mourning for the end of his high school years so I used my soft voice. "Take your time, sweetie, and be sure you feel good about your choices. I booked four hours for this. What ~~will we do until our mani/pedi at 3:30~~ is your hurry?

Alex: Black

Sales clerk: That'll be $185. Damage it and it doubles.

Me: It's been a pleasure having you ~~rob me blind in under ten minutes~~ help us, good sir!

The shopping trip I'd been waiting for my entire life took literally seven minutes. You heard me. There was no sobbing, no screaming matches, and not even a mention of the spray tan appointment I had made for him.

Then, just as I slipped my credit card back into my wallet something totally awesome happened—our sweet boy looked up from his iPhone (just joking! Ha ha!) and almost looked at me. Jealous much?? I welled up at the obvious emotion he was trying to hide from me, his giver of life. Then he said something poignant which made up for the total letdown of a day. He mumbled, "Let's get outta here."

I perked up, "OMG, yes!! I'd love to! Let's go for a latte and some hazelnut biscotti and gush about your tux!! I love you, my sweet boy!" This time he looked at me for reals. He wiped ~~tears~~ crusty sleep from his eyes and said, "Nah. Home." I responded, "Oooh, okay—you want to go home because I've made it the most special place in the world for you, right??"

Crickets. . .

As I tried to sleep that night, I replayed the day in my head. I got excited when I counted *nineteen* words my boy had said at the clothing store—well, only fourteen if you count 'black' because he said it like...five times. Plus, he looked at me that one time! Just because he didn't cry or say he looked fat or beg to go for a mani/pedi afterwards doesn't mean it was a total bust. Just kidding!! Yes it does.

FYI—I've booked off next week to shop for my *Miss World* gown. All I know is this—it will be a chiffon fitted number with spaghetti straps and a twelve-foot train. And it won't be ~~stupid~~ black.

Emergency Shirt

Two years after Alex brought shame upon our family by ruining tux shopping, it was time for Max to ~~finish me off~~ graduate. I had held out hope that he would act ~~like a girl~~ appropriately when it came to life's turning points, but all his grad year did was dredge up ugly memories. Like his brother, his priorities were totally whacked.

In early October, Max casually looked up from his iPhone (Just joking-ha! Ha!) and mumbled, "Grad pics tomorrow."

"Tomorrow??! Over my totally ripped dead body! You need a haircut, a new shirt and a spray tan!!"

What he said next will haunt me to my grave, "Nah."

"What in God's name ~~is your problem~~ will you wear??" I shrieked.

"The photographer has an emergency shirt and tie, Mom. It's chill."

Emergency shirt?? I'd heard of an emergency C-section, an emergency family meeting, and an emergency Cabernet Sauvignon, but never, ever an *emergency shirt*! Would Jon Hamm or Justin Timberlake ever be caught in an *emergency shirt*? Then neither should my loinfruit!

I was the only rational one in the household obviously. "Max. You don't know if this *emergency shirt* will fit you. Forget it. I'm going to the mall… which closes in sixteen ~~#$%ing~~ minutes!"

On my way out the door he said something horrible—"Mom, it's not a **real** shirt. It's a fake collar you just haul over your hoodie. It doesn't have to fit."

At the thought of my flesh and blood posing in a mildewed, once-white shirt and the photo being ~~leaked to People magazine~~ sent out with our Christmas cards, I felt super faint and inhaled ~~a pitcher of emergency shooters~~ deeply to settle myself down. Then I asked one more question to be sure I understood what was happening.

"Is there an emergency tie, and, if so, will it match the *emergency shirt*?"

"Dunno. Doesn't matter. Nobody cares about that stuff."

Time stood still after he said those terrible words. I angrily pointed at my *Miss World* vision board, and, in a trembling voice, I screamed, "What did you just say to me? Should I order a DNA test right this minute because, hand to God, I'm not sure you're mine! You've literally made me ashamed of you. What do you think the point of graduating is?? You're making it sound like it's about moving onto the next phase of your life you get photoshopped and airbrushed every day, when in actual fact this happens like—never! Look me in my hazel, gold-speckled eyes, and tell me you don't like the paparazzi getting your picture taken. Say it!!"

I think I finally got through to him because he looked up from his iPhone (Kidding!! Ha! Ha!) and mumbled, "Whatever. Gawd, Mom. Calm down." Sometimes you have to go for the jugular to make them understand what really matters in this super dark world.

The pictures turned out perfectly, thank God!! Max and I had a good chat about priorities, and I said stuff like, "Look, you know I'm proud of you and super happy you're graduating and going off to pursue an awesome career path, but—let's get real—there is no point to any of it without airbrushed photos. Let's put this behind us and pretend it never happened, okay, sweetie?"

It didn't seem like the right time to tell him that, in no uncertain terms, he was getting a spray tan for grad prom. I was too exhausted from trying to make our sons into girls see the light! How had things gotten so screwed up in this family?? Sigh. Sometimes I wondered if our sons even knew they had royalty in their blood.

Do-Over

With the grad photo shoot nightmare behind us, it was prom time again! I was getting a do-over!! Woot! My buzz-kill of a therapist warned me to manage my expectations (Blah. Blah. Blah.) this time, but I was hell-bent on making some beautiful grad/prom memories with Max. Bring on the soul-crushing shopping trips, mother/son heart to hearts, and second mortgage to pay for the awesome fighter jet that would deposit him on the roof of his high school on prom night while his jealous friends looked on. Boom.

During the first week of school, Max came home one afternoon and actually used the word 'prom' in a sentence. I was totally psyched…until he finished the sentence. Here's what he said: "Get this, Mom—the girls in my class are shopping for their prom dresses already. It's like ten months away. So dope."

I was all like, "Yea, really. I hate spending quality time at the mall in fluorescent-bathed stores drooling over dresses and then going for a delicious lunch and dissecting each and every dress in detail. Duh. So dope."

Between September and June there was so much to do! I had to unfriend people on Facebook who uploaded mother/daughter prom dress shopping selfies and remodel the kitchen for when Max decided at the last minute he wanted a grad party. The tension was super thick. I spent endless nights tossing and turning, wondering when would be the right time to tell our son he might need a ~~pedicure~~ haircut before prom. I worried that he, too, was lying awake at night fretting, but he was brave and didn't let on.

The last two weeks of June, I was an emotional wreck as I tried to piece together the final details. For instance, prom was weeks away, and Max hadn't chosen a tux. I had learnt from his older brother's tux-shopping experience not to ~~scream and threaten~~ expect much, so I kept it cool and said, "Hey. I wonder if we should go tux shopping soon. It's no biggie—only takes like five minutes. Maybe we could grab some wings after. Whatevs. ~~Mommy loves you to the moon and back.~~"

Max: I picked it out yesterday. I went with *the boys.*

Me: How did you know ~~this would be the final straw for me~~ what to do without me, sweetie?

Max: I need sixty bucks for two prom tickets.

Me: Oh! ~~I'd be honored to go with you, sweet little man!~~ Who are you taking to prom??

Max: You don't know her.

Me: OMG, what's her name? What's she like? How did you meet her? Has she been in a pageant before??

Max: I'm starving. When's supper?

Me: What about a corsage?? I can pick it up for you!

Max: What's a corsage?

Me: I need to know the style of your date's dress.

Max: Pink

Me: Style, not color! OMG. Is it strapless?

Max: Dunno

Me: I'll just get a wrist corsage. It's perfect for any dress style, and probably what I'll wear in the *Miss World* pageant FYI.

Max: What's for supper?

The emotions were ~~non-existent~~ taking a toll. On prom day, I went to work like it was any other normal day, but I was a total wreck. I hoped Max would remember to brush his teeth, so I texted him a reminder—*Don't forget to brush your teeth, sweetie, and remember to tell your date she looks almost as pretty as your beauty queen mother.*

He didn't respond, and I remembered I had to ask questions. Duh.

Me: Are you okay with your bowtie?

Max: Ya

Me: Is it pretied?

Max: Ya

Me: What time are you leaving?

Max: Idk (I don't know)

Me: Where are you guys going for photos?

Max: Olivia's

Me: Where does she live?

Max: When's supper? I'm starving.

He seemed confused, and I was terrified he was having ~~another~~ stroke, so I raced home. What I saw when I walked through the door will haunt me until my last breath. There he was in his tux, standing over the sink eating his fifth hot dog. I'd ~~done~~ seen this a million times. It was classic—stuffing yourself with food to dull the emotions. He needed me, and he didn't even know it, bless his precious little heart.

Me: Mommy's here. Do you need to talk? Do you have any questions about
stuff we may not have covered—like how to do the tango?? We can
practice right now—I have dancing shoes. It'll be super awesome,
sweetie.

Max: Are we outta ketchup?

Me: Does that mean we're not doing the tango? Whatever. I didn't feel like it
anyway. Wipe the crumbs off your tux.

Then he left for photos without a backward glance or a hot dog bun crumb trail that I could follow.

I hacked into his Snapchat account until I found out where the pictures were being taken. Boom. When we arrived at the sprawling lawn covered with gorgeous adolescent couples dressed in finery that I could only afford if I went back to being a ~~stripper~~ waitress on the side, I spotted our handsome baby boy. He walked over to us!! OMG. Obviously, he wanted to spend a few hours chit chatting with his giver of life! He almost looked me in the eye as he spoke, "I forgot my sneakers for the party after prom. Can you go get them?" I got choked up knowing he still needed me, and I hardly even noticed the mothers French-braiding their daughters' hair on a ~~stupid~~ blanket on the ~~stupid~~ lawn. French braids are totally out of style by the way.

~~Losers.~~

After I dutifully fetched his sneakers, my husband and I drove straight to the high school to get ~~a hundred~~ more pics of our baby boy before he went into prom. As the teens pulled up in their fancy sports cars, I remembered fondly how I had arrived at my prom in a hay baler. By the time he and his date arrived, my hair was total crap, but my dress still rocked it, so I pulled Max aside for a few family shots. After the fifty-ninth photo, he got all huffy when I said, "Rest your head on my shoulder for this one, k?" And "Smile with your eyes, sweetie!" Then he mumbled something that sounded like, "Please leave now" but it couldn't have been that because I'm his giver of life. Note to self—get hearing checked. Ha! Ha!

I'd never say it to Max, but I'm glad it's over. As ~~unfulfilling~~ as prom planning was, it was super ~~boring~~ exhausting. Also, I've got to save some energy for being mother of the groom one day. I hear they get to ~~be invisible~~ sit at a special table. Sounds so ~~lame~~ awesome!

I Am Literally a Dog Whisperer

I've never owned a dog mainly because they make messes, eat and ~~breathe~~ poop non-stop, and I've had enough of that with teenagers, thank you very much. When a dear friend asked me to dogsit Jak, her Wheaton Terrier, I was hesitant to have another non-verbal, messy male in the house. But, because I ~~was mainlining Merlot at the time~~ am a super giving person, I agreed to it.

When my friend showed up with Jak I was filled with ~~regret~~ questions:

How often does he eat? Can he be left alone for three days? Where are his slippers so he doesn't make tracks on the floor? Where are his pants so he doesn't sit his bare butt on my couch after he poops?

After my ~~weird~~ friend stopped laughing at my non-funny questions, she left, pretending she trusted me with her canine. The first night went okay, except for the window cleaner he drank by mistake. How was I supposed to know he'd think it was his water just because it was in a bowl on the floor??? Not my fault.

Dog Lesson #1: Foaming at the mouth and playing dead are serious business. When this happens, (and it does all the time, I'm sure, to everyone who has dogs. Duh.) you shouldn't just keep throwing a ball at them and saying, "Fetch, dummy!"

After the window cleaner incident, Jak seemed ~~edgy and distrustful~~ to settle into our household. Thanks to Google and YouTube, I learned that when dogs scratch at the door, they need to go outside, and when they point at their mouths and bark ~~for five hours,~~ they are super hungry. By the end of the first day, I was literally the Dog Whisperer. Jealous much?

Jak felt ~~betrayed by his owners~~ it too. In no time flat, we developed a mutual respect. Every time I would walk toward his dog food and yell "~~Psych!! Ha ha~~ Here, Jak!" he would wag his tail and give me eye contact. Because I hadn't had eye contact since our boys became teenagers, I went overboard with gratitude and made him my ~~sole beneficiary~~ famous chocolate chip cookies. I wish I'd Googled 'should dogs eat chocolate?' before he ate seven-

~~teen~~ of them, but thankfully he didn't vomit for too long. Phew.

Also, when I gave Jak a command, he did it without talking back, mumbling 'Just a sec', or rolling his eyes!! When I said, "Sit, Jak!", he sat! I was stoked that someone did what I asked, so I rewarded him by reading P.D. Eastman's *Go, Dog, Go!* even though he kept wriggling out of the blanket I'd swaddled him in.

After a few days with the cuddly canine, I realized I had had it all wrong. Yes, dogs are a bit of work, but, when they sniff your super toned butt and stare deep into your awesome and pure soul, it's totally worth it!! Literally, no one in my household does those things. Jak met my needs and made me ~~a Mother's Day card~~ feel good. Check out the differences between dogs and teens, and you'll see why I ~~drink~~ fell in love with Jak.

Here's Jak giving me some hard-core eye contact:

Here's Max giving eye contact:

Here's Jak's room: *Annnnd Max's room:*

*Jak looking sheepish after being told
to settle down*

*Max looking sheepish after my
lecture on too much texting*

Jak waiting patiently for his tiny treats that he won't eat before he hears, "Take it, Jak":

Max waiting patiently for supper when I say, "Supper will be ready in 30 seconds!!! Shut that #$%ing fridge door!"

Jak being told to go to bed

Max listening intently as I suggest he stop texting and get some sleep

And here's one that shows Jak's *Girls' Night Out* side. It was our last night together. We reminisced a lot, and he even ~~slept through it~~ whimpered ~~when I swaddled him for our fifth story book~~. "There, there, Jak. It's okay," I said. "Your real owners love you even though you obviously prefer me or why else would you be on my lap ~~against your will~~? Duh." Once I finished the whole bottle of Pinot Grigio, he seemed to feel better. I did too.

When my friend came to get Jak the next day, he ran to her like ~~he'd been abused for crissake~~ I didn't exist anymore. Pfft. Turns out Jak is fickle as hell, and I was nothing more than someone to feed and clean up after him, so how is that different than my life pre-Jak?? As he wagged his tail and hopped into the car without one second of eye contact, I yelled, "~~Take your stupid Mother's Day card which is just a bunch of dog food smeared on paper as far as I can tell~~! Bye, Jak! Let's always remember the good times!"

Once the fickle little bugger left, I was super enraged to see paw prints all over my hardwood floors—I felt totally used. Even if I was literally a dog whisperer, it doesn't mean I needed another living creature to clean up after. The eye contact, unconditional love, and butt sniffing were awesome, but clean floors are also amazing. Plus, I'll get more than enough eye contact from fans once I'm *Miss World*. Pfft. Jak. Schmak.

Section 3

I Was a Super ~~Neurotic~~ Mom
Even After the Boys Moved Out

After parenting my firstborn for eighteen years, I hated like hell that he ~~still didn't know my name~~ was going off on his own, without me, his giver of life! When Alex was ready to depart for university and leave the perfect nest I'd created for him (Fine. Leave the perfect nest I made for you. See if I care.), I literally panicked. I just didn't know if we ~~would ever get our car back~~ had taught our little man everything he needed to make it without us in this harsh world. I wondered if maybe I should have allowed him to ~~cut his own steak~~ figure more things out on his own. Nah—then he wouldn't have needed me. Duh.

It felt too late for a family meeting to highlight the things I may have neglected (Don't run with scissors. Call Mommy every day…) so I decided instead to write him some last-minute advice to help him through university without Mommy:

☺ Don't throw away your clothes when they get dirty. Look for a washing machine (Google it) and ~~pretend you've used one before~~ follow the instructions on the inside of the lid.

☺ When you notice white flakes in the sky and cold white stuff on the ground, that means it is winter. This means ~~you should skip classes like I did and stay warm~~ it is very cold. Wear a jacket ~~or wrap yourself in the fleece blanket I gave you and call me so I can read you a story.~~ (Google it). PS Jackets and hoodies are not the same thing.

☺ Wash your bed sheets weekly. The fitted sheet (Google it) is the one with elasticized corners and is tricky to fold (YouTube it). If the tight elastic snaps and gives you a boo boo, call me right away. Mommy's never far away.

☺ Drinking alcohol is a ~~total blast~~ bad idea. Stick with milk or maybe juice if you feel like letting loose, but not the overly sugary kinds because sugar is very bad for you, sweet man.

☺ Look for a girlfriend with a tiara.

☺ Please accept my Facebook friend request so I can ~~creep you~~ see fun pics of you, sweetie! Plus, I'm always available for private Facebook messages. Just fire me off a daily message, and I'll get back to you immediately.

Promise. xoxo

Just to be totally sure he'd be okay, I tattooed our home address and code word ('Queen') for 'stranger danger' on his wrist. I had to accept that I'd done the best I could. Clearly it wasn't good enough because he was leaving the perfect nest I'd made for him. Pfft. Didn't care except when I was awake.

Mommy's on Her Way!

Some people say that I over-parent and have a hard time cutting the ~~umbilical~~ cord. To those people I say, ~~"Shut your #$%ing pie hole!"~~ "I prefer to call it 'nurturing' thank you very much." ~~Smothering~~ Loving your kids is hardly over-parenting! In Alex's first year at university, he texted me one February day with the most beautiful message I've ever received: *Hey. I've been sick for a week. Thinking of coming home for a few days.*

I put down my wine glass and texted him back: *I am sorry to hear this, sweetie* ☺☹. *Hang tight! Mommy's on her way, little man! xoxoxo*

I called my husband with the awesome news, and we argued over who would fetch Alex. Phil won because he put the fake police lights on the car roof and sped past me going 150 kph. Jerk. While he outran the cops, I raced to the pharmacy and loaded up on Sinutab, Neo-Citron, and an infra-red sauna so our boy could sweat out the flu in comfort. If I had to go back to pole dancing at night to offset the costs of keeping my son alive, so be it. Judge yourself, Miss Umbilical Cord Cutter!

The minute our six-foot baby boy dragged himself through the front door, I grabbed a stepladder so I could reach his forehead to check for a fever. He was burning up. Boom. This was awesome news! I piggybacked him to his bed, fluffed his pillows, administered flu meds, and warmed up his ~~ba-ba (bottle)~~ room. He seemed a little hungry, so I made his favorite comfort food—~~strained peaches~~ grilled cheese. While he dozed off I read ~~Good Night, Moon to him~~ about homeopathic decongestants on the Inter-web thingy. I even said he could wear my tiara just this one time, but he pretended to be asleep. Whatever.

When days later, he finally slept through the night, hacked up a huge mucous ball, and said "Bye, Mom!", I knew he was going to live...because of me obviously. I sent him off with a suitcase full of pharmaceuticals, clean clothes, and ~~a framed photo of me~~ some vitamins. Then I stood in the driveway waving good-bye until Phil pointed out, "He's been gone for an hour. You're making a fool of yourself."

Go ahead. Let your child waste away from flu complications by all means. If your idea of over-parenting is me nursing my precious baby boy back to health, getting extra airbags installed in his car, and tying his shoe-laces, then by all means sign me up for *Over-Parenters Anonymous*. Now, if you'll excuse me, I have things to do such as ironing ~~bibs~~ my evening gown and sash.

Fine. Leave the Perfect Nest I Made for You. See if I Care

Faced with my last kick at the parenting can, I tried to brace myself for our younger son's departure for university. Max, like his brother, seemed excited to leave home for whatever ~~stupid~~ reason. (Fine. Leave the perfect nest I made for you. See if I care.) Obviously, I hoped to share every detail of this awesome adventure with him. I wanted to help him choose a funky comforter for his residence room. I wanted ~~him to act like a girl~~ to go for long walks with him and hear about his hopes and dreams, but mostly I wanted him to look ~~up from his cell phone~~ to me for guidance during this devastating life transition.

For the two days leading up to his move to campus, I literally had mental ~~breakdowns~~ telepathy. I was out of town, but I sensed Max wasn't getting ready for moving day. Before leaving, I had reminded him to do his laundry, so we could start packing. He strummed his guitar and nodded. To be sure he'd heard me, I texted him later that evening. I kept it loose and friendly, so he wouldn't feel sad about leaving the perfect nest I made for him:

Me: Hi sweetie. What did you do today? ~~Say 'laundry' or I'll drive off a bridge I swear to God~~.

Max: Not much

Me: Please remember to do your laundry and I'll help you pack tomorrow ok? Don't forget.

Max: Yah

The tone of his text was super ~~un~~reassuring. I knew he was doing ~~SFA~~ stuff to get ready for his move and I had ~~lots~~ nothing to worry about. I slept like a ~~colicky~~ baby that night. The next day I checked in again:

Me: Hi ~~precious little man~~. How ~~will you live without Mommy~~ are things going?

Max: Good

Me: What are you doing?

Max: Just hangin'

Me: Did you do your laundry yet? ~~Say 'yes' or I'll drive off a bridge I swear to God.~~

Max: Nah. I will. Chill.

Me: You leave tomorrow…Are you going to be ready ~~to live without mommy~~??

Max: Yah

When I arrived home at 5 p.m. on the night before moving day, I noticed something horrible—he hadn't done his laundry.

Obviously, there would be no time to look through photo albums together, which I had scheduled between 7-9 p.m.!! I had to change my whole schedule, and it was going to be tough to find last-minute bonding time with my baby boy! Grrrr. Here's the ~~stupid~~ revised schedule:

5:05: I ~~Google directions to the nearest bridge~~ say, "Max, you have to do your laundry so we can pack, sweetie."

5:30: I say, "Max, you have to do your laundry so we can pack, sweetie."

5:45: I say, "Max you have to do your ~~mother @#$ing~~ laundry so we can pack, sweetie."

6:00: He's obviously texting his friends to say he's literally a wreck because he's leaving me. Poor little fella.☹

6:30: Max says, "Goin' to the mall to get binders." I say, "Ooohh, want me to come with you, sweetie?" He says "Nah." Pfft. Didn't want to anyway!

7:30: He returns home with five binders and some pens.

7:45: He finally throws in a super large load of multi-coloured garments and presses the HOT button. I am surprised ~~I've survived to this point~~ he's taking ownership!

8:30: He puts his clothes in the dryer and takes a much needed break because he's literally exhausted after pressing two buttons.

8:40: I say, "Please ~~drive me to the nearest bridge~~ put in another load and fold the first one, sweetie."

8:45: I say, "Please ~~drive me to the nearest bridge~~ put in another @#$ing load and fold the first one, sweetie."

8:50: Phil puts his foot down.

9:15: I get out the bag of toiletries I bought for my baby boy.

9:30: Max finally gets emotional: "Did you remember to buy razors?" I choke up, obviously, and say, "When did my baby start shaving??"

9:45: Max throws his worldly goods into garbage bags and says something totally profound, "There. Done." I reach for more Kleenex.

The next morning, he raced out of bed at 11:30 a.m. As I watched Max inhale his eighth bowl of Cheerios, I flashed back to my first day of university. I had sobbed inconsolably when I left my mother, so I braced myself for the tears that were coming. Zoom in and you'll notice his bottom lip is about to tremble. Can't see it?? What are you talking about? You must literally be blind.

We loaded up the truck. During the drive to university, I gave Max one last chance to share his feelings with me. I asked how he was feeling, and if he felt excited about this new chapter in his life. He finally unleashed, "Good" and "Yup". Don't be jealous. Your kids probably share their feelings with you too.

After we dropped him off, helped him unpack, organized his room, purchased his books, bought him snacks for his room, ~~burped him,~~ and paid his residence fees, my husband and I declared ~~bankruptcy~~ it was time to go. Max walked ~~two feet in front of us~~ us out. We hugged him, and I told him to text ~~hourly~~ if he needed anything. He ~~ran really fast~~ walked back to his residence and pretended not to hear as I hollered, "Wait! You forgot your Thomas the Tank Engine lunch box, sweetie! We love you, special little man! Good luck!"

On the drive home, I checked my phone to see if he'd texted. He hadn't. Obviously, his battery had died. Duh. As I tucked my phone into my purse, I got a speck of stupid dust in my eye, and had to wear my sunglasses all the way ~~to the nearest bridge~~ home. Stupid ~~milestones~~ dust.

I'm ~~Not~~ an Amazing Interior Designer

Remember how my creative sandwich making literally got my kid into medical school? I left out the horrible part—the medical school is in another province! When I found out, I totally wished I had cut his sandwiches into regular triangles! Why did I have to be so amazing, and, as a result, singlehandedly push my son away from me, his giver of life?

As he was packing for Toronto, he masked his true feelings by saying weird stuff like, *I can't wait to move to Toronto!* While he packed for our massive road trip, I went back to what I did best—making sandwiches and I can tell you I cut them in triangles. I wasn't about to make the same mistake twice!

On the seven million-kilometre drive to Toronto, I wracked my brain for ways to make Alex need me one last time. Sure, packing sandwiches was an awesome idea even though my family ignored me when I said, *Hey, why are we stopping at Subway? I spent an hour making sandwiches. Remember, guys?* They played deaf and ordered four *footlongs* while my sandwiches rotted in the cooler because I forgot ice packs. ~~Idiots~~.

There had to be something meaningful I could contribute besides screaming, *I gave up my six-pack abs to bring you into this world and this is how you repay me?? By moving halfway across the country??* Sixteen thousand hours later, we arrived at his apartment on campus, and it became super clear how I could help—he was obviously going to need my designer know-how. Boom. The place was in desperate need of some ~~fumigating~~ TLC. I was going to show my boy how to make a house an awesome home, if it was the last thing I did. I imagined the possibilities to jazz things up: plants, pictures, marble countertops, and a customized Italian glass backsplash at the very least.

On my way out the door to Walmart to begin the unscripted HGTV special, I asked him, "Would you like some pictures for your walls?"

He couldn't contain his excitement. "Nah."

Me: How about a few plants?

Alex: Nah. They'll die.

Me: A bowlful of potpourri? Wicker baskets? Slipcovers for those chairs?? A robin's egg blue accent wall?

Alex: I don't understand ~~why you're still here~~ anything you just said.

Sigh. Words weren't working. I had to **show** him the possibilities, so on our third ~~hundredth~~ trip to Walmart, I dragged him to the home décor section and pointed out irresistible things like:

Or maybe this to make the walls pop:

Awwww… Remember this, sweetie??

He couldn't decide so he said, "~~Get some help~~. Nah."

Beauty queens are persistent as hell, so I took it upon myself to slip a cinnamon-scented candle into the shopping cart. That got his attention!

Alex: Uh. What's that?

Me: Duh. It's a cinnamon-scented candle, you precious goofball! The smell will hopefully remind you of that Christmas we made that gingerbread house. It took over two hours, and the roof slid off and the walls fell over, and ~~I yelled, "I hate you, Martha @#$ing Stewart!!"~~ we laughed until our tummies hurt. Remember, sweetie??

Crickets. . .

As he ~~ran away from me~~ went in search of an Ethernet cable (boooorrring!), I grabbed a floor lamp and a plaid throw pillow. This was on.

Back at the apartment I fussed for ~~seconds~~ hours, while the guys tried to set up the TV (boooorrring!) Ta da!

Nailed it right?! I know!

The guys were all like, "Mom, ~~you killed it~~! We're starved."

Once they finally stopped ~~barely acknowledging~~ gushing over my decorating genius, I had to remind Alex of the throw cushion rules:

☻ Do not sit on it. Ever. Promise me.

☻ Fluff it up every time you walk by it. Promise me.

My work there was done obviously. As I turned toward the door to leave, I took one last glimpse at my handsome, towering son. It was clear he ~~had already squished the damn cushion~~ was no longer the little boy who needed notes from his awesome giver of life. But I left him one just the same:

Have a good semester, sweet little man! See you soon. You will become a doctor one day for reals.

PS Call me ~~every day to say you miss me~~ if you have questions about cushion fluffing or beauty pageants.

PPS The cinnamon-scented candle is in your top kitchen drawer beside the floral-patterned oven mitts. Light it when you're lonely for me and I'll light one for you too.

Love, Mom xox

"I Will Navr Leve You Momy"—Filthy Liars!

I literally don't get it. I'd spent my entire life building a perfect nest for our boys, and then one day without warning, they were all like—*I want to go to university and do great things in the world.* When I heard that, I was like—*Why are you doing this to me?? What in God's actual name did I do to make it so unbearable here that you have to go and spread your wings and conquer the world? Answer me, you ungrateful little—!*

Well, guess what? When Max decided to follow his brother's footsteps and leave the perfect nest I'd made for him, I handled it just fine, once I got out of rehab.

Obviously there was an adjustment period, but show me one devoted mother out there who *hasn't* texted her beloved sons hourly to let them know she's always there for them:

Hi, sweet little man! Look out your window!! Surprise!! Mommy's waving at you right now. xo ☺.

Also, digging up Mother's Day cards your kids made for you thirteen years ago which clearly stated they would never leave you (*I wil navr leve you momy. I lov you so mutsh*) and screaming, "Filthy liars!!!" is hardly unusual behavior for someone who's been tossed aside. But eventually I simmered down and started to see the benefits of the absence of ~~messy~~ teenagers who address me as *Hey* rather than showing me the respect I deserve by calling me ~~Miss Nackawic 1981~~ Queen Mom. Pfft. Good riddance.

Here are a few of the perks I discovered after my children left the perfect nest that I'd created for them:

🐶 I could finally do my signature *Naked Downward Facing Dog* pose anywhere in the house without our hyper-sensitive boys running from the room screaming that their "mommy issues" were all my fault and that I should "get some help". I honestly don't miss the drama.

🐶 Phil and I could go to Mexico once/month with the money we saved on groceries and hockey gear. Kidding! We could go once/week. Boom.

🐶 A balanced meal was now one where I could balance my plate in one hand and my wine glass in the other. Just because I sometimes forgot to put food on my actual plate did not for one second mean I needed another intervention, so worry about yourself for a change!

😌 I could explore new hobbies, intellectual pursuits, and creative outlets. According to recent studies, napping *is so* a hobby. If done correctly, it most certainly *can* lead to intellectual pursuits and creative outlets. Just because *you* enjoy painting pastoral settings or feeding the homeless, it doesn't mean I have to—so, by all means, go save the world! Pfft.

😌 No more school-related meetings where I would waste an entire hour texting my BFFs and getting weird, annoying looks from committee members for exercising my God-given right to state my opinion: *This is super boring, you guys. Can we wrap it up?* Fine. Choose people who have no opinions. OMG.

See? Being abandoned by your loinfruits despite creating a perfect nest for them doesn't necessarily spell Ativan the end of the world. Can I level with you, though? Now that I have time on my hands, I find myself putting off Miss World-related tasks such as updating my Miss World vision board, finding the perfect open-toed sandal, and practising my acceptance speech.

This is gonna sound super crazy, but my life coach said I might be scared to fail and that is why I'm procrastinating. I laughed in her jealous face… But then I got to thinking, if, after all this work, I only land *First Princess* or worse—*Miss Congeniality*—I swear to God, my entire life will have been a total waste. Psych!! Ha! Ha! Of course I'll win the big title! Duh. Until then I'll keep shooting myself in the foot for the stars. I'm going to use my new-found freedom to go hard at my dream… after my nap. Obviously.

Section 4

I'm Totally ~~Not~~ Rocking Midlife. Boom

Seeking Wider Horizons Until I Win Miss World

A few years ago my father visited and brought with him a box filled with my childhood memories. He said, "I ~~put this crap by the curb and no one took it~~ thought you might like some of this stuff." My diary from grade ~~twelve~~ five was the first thing I noticed—the cover was bedazzled and the pages were filled with super loopy penmanship and swirly hearts. Each of the three-hundred pages had a clear theme—*I want to be pretty. I want to be popular. I want to be a famous beauty queen.* Pfft. Who cares that I haven't reached my childhood goals yet. Some things take time. Also, who cares if other people have weird dreams that don't even make sense—like climbing Mount Everest or being in an Ironman competition. Who would sacrifice their hair for such ridiculous ventures?! Not me, that's who.

I'll never give up on my dream of being a famous beauty queen, especially when it's obviously within my grasp and probably just around the next corner. In the meantime though, I pledge to seek wider horizons, which is expected of any *Miss World* worth her salt. I wrote a few Bucket List goals to keep me focused until the big day:

☻ Climb the highest ~~mountain~~ social ladder I can find.

☻ Master the perfect ~~soufflé~~ Smoky Cat Eye .

☻ Learn how to speak ~~French~~ super good in front of judges and an audience.

☻ Swim ~~the English Channel~~ at the local pool in a string bikini.

☻ Visit at least one of the ~~Seven Wonders~~ bridal boutiques in town for my pageant gown.

Boom. I have my work cut out for me. This list really made me see that I *am* about more than the pageant I'm going to win, and I hope young girls reading this will aim for bigger things too! I didn't even know this was going to be an inspirational list when I started it! Maybe I have more gifts than I realize, and I should become a motivational speaker?!! OMG that could be my talent!!!

Mammogram: A Total Day at the Spa

Being middle-aged is totally ~~crappy~~ awesome for many reasons. One of my favourites is the yearly mammogram, which is a must after a certain age. I wish mammograms were monthly because they're like a day at the spa— and they're free! Boom.

When I step inside the hospital I feel like ~~writing my obituary~~ I've died and gone to heaven—the ~~fluorescent~~ soft lighting, the smell of ~~fecal waste~~ lavender, and the soothing sounds of ~~Code Blue~~ Mozart wafting through the speakers. My body goes super ~~rigid~~ limp with ~~fear~~ relaxation.

Next, an awesome hospital volunteer will personally escort—you heard me—personal escort—you to the waiting area. Upper crust, or what?? Try not to stare too much because you'll literally be begging for the interior decorator's phone number. The place is filled with ~~ugly~~ funky plastic chairs and ~~posters of cancer warnings~~ fine art. Also, the people lined up against the wall on stretchers are super friendly, especially the ones who are ~~alive~~ awake. It's a ~~cold and sterile~~ warm and welcoming atmosphere all the way around.

Just when you think it can't get any better, you'll be instructed to enter a cozy ~~2x2~~ locker to slip into your very own ~~scratchy~~ designer robe!! Eeeeee! The only other places where they give you a robe are hotels and suites on cruise ships. Just sayin'. The robe's a head-turner—one millimetre thick, grey and baby blue, with seventeen ties that make you feel like you're in a ~~strait-jacket~~ fashion show! Those fashionable ties are just for looks though. They don't keep your robe closed, but, when your boobies fall out, you might make some new friends!

The real fun begins when the mammogram technician calls your name. She'll sit you down and ask you some 'getting to know you' questions: *When was your last period? Have you noticed any changes in your breasts? How often do you perform a breast self-exam?* (Daily. Wink. Wink.) It's super obvious that she needs friends because she asks like a million totally personal questions. Some people are just lonely and a bit nosy I guess.

After the chit chat she'll tape funky mammogram markers to your nipples. Now it's a party!

Two words: pizza party. The technician will handle your breasts like lumps of fresh dough. Just when you think she's going to toss them into the air and yell, "Mama Mia, Pizzeria!" she will slap one down onto a cold steel plate and tell you to take a deep breath. What a jokester! Ha! Ha! You both know it's impossible to breathe because the cold metal plate already sucked the breath out of you!

It's super normal if you start humming James Taylor's *Steamroller* when the 8-billion-pound press flattens your boobies into the thickness of a *Miss World* sash. The technician will remind you it's very important not to move. When mine says this, I always say, "You're so funny, Deb. I'm trapped here and literally can't move, but I just love your goofy humour." When the death vice releases your ~~mangled~~ breast, don't be sad because guess what? You get three more x-rays. Surprise! Two per side. Boom.

The whole thing takes about fifteen minutes, and you'll feel so ~~sore~~ refreshed when it's over. The worst part is having to give back that ~~scratchy~~ designer robe but don't forget—you'll get to slip it on again next time! Put the party favours/mammogram nipple markers in your purse as a little reminder of your getaway and the importance of doing this regularly. Pat yourself on the back for ~~surviving~~ getting a mammogram, and go treat yourself to something special like a tiara-wearing night out with your friends.

Shoot! I keep forgetting that not everyone has a tiara. Just me. Oh well.

Night Sweats

Once or twice ~~per night~~ since turning a certain age (which is none of your beeswax) I've been awakened by the horrible sensation of drowning… because I was…in my own ~~#$%ing~~ perspiration. It's something that my ~~oblivious and selfish~~ loving husband doesn't have to endure, and it's imperative that my suffering not be a burden to him. After my ~~nightly~~ occasional night sweats, I felt compelled to compile a list of tips to help women deal with them in a quiet and unselfish way:

☽ Towel off, take a quick shower, and change the sopping wet bed sheets. Gently ~~punch~~ nudge your ~~oblivious and selfish~~ loving partner awake so he can ~~suffer~~ enjoy the fresh sheets too.

☽ Read ~~aloud~~ using a tiny ~~strobe~~ light until you feel sleepy, but be careful not to wake your ~~oblivious and selfish~~ loving partner by shining the light into his eyes. My guy hates that, and I honestly keep forgetting! Ha! Ha! Oh well.

☽ Meditate. If you have terrible and unwanted thoughts like how you haven't moved forward in your life, or that people are taking things that are rightfully yours (*Miss Worlds 1982-2017*), simply acknowledge those thoughts and come back to the present moment. If the thoughts continue, just ~~swear like a trucker~~ sigh loudly, but do not wake your ~~oblivious and selfish~~ loving partner to blame him for everything that's gone wrong in your life. My guy hates that, and I honestly keep forgetting! Ha! Ha!! Oh well.

☽ Belly breathe. Inhale deeply and expand your belly with each breath. It can be discouraging to see your pageant-worthy, ~~muffin top~~ six-pack abs stretched so far from your actual spine, so try to just find a spot on the wall and focus on that instead. Hold the breath for eight seconds, and then exhale with such force that your curtains actually move and you spray your ~~oblivious and selfish~~ loving partner with spittle. Oooppps!! Ha! Ha! Oh well.

☽ Sprinkle your pillows with ~~rum~~ lavender essential oil, which has a soothing effect. If that doesn't work, put the bottle close to your nose, and take three deep ~~gulps~~ breaths so it works quicker. Boom. You'll be out in no time.

☙ Try a little yoga move called *Legs up the Wall*. Lie on your back on the floor and lift your legs up the wall. It might feel weird at first, especially if you're not wearing underwear and your butt is against a heater that's burning hot, but stick with it because the pose lowers blood pressure, relieves tension, slows breathing, and allows you to ~~see how filthy your window blinds are~~ settle down and relax.

☙ Say 'Ohm' twenty times in a range low and loud enough to scare the pattern off your duvet. There is nothing like the soothing sound of 'Ohm' repeated over and over from the bowels of your vocal cords to settle racing thoughts. If, for some weird reason, your ~~oblivious and selfish~~ loving partner wakes up, apologize and reassure him that your inability to sleep is hardly his problem and that you sincerely hope he goes straight ~~to hell~~ back to sleep. Asking for forgiveness is good for a marriage.

I sincerely hope these tips help anyone suffering from night sweats, but more than that I hope that ~~oblivious and selfish~~ loving partners of suffering women will not lose sleep needlessly. I also sincerely hope I have a giant bed with breathable, 850 thread count sheets all to myself at the upcoming *Miss World* pageant.

Menopause...Pfft. As if

News flash: Just because *some* women over the age of ~~fifty~~ forty have hormonal mood swings does not for one second mean I am one of them. Furthermore, just because I laugh, cry and take the occasional ~~hostage~~ hissy fit within a fifteen-minute period doesn't for one second qualify me as menopausal or moody—it simply means I am super passionate and animated. Menopause... Pfft. As *if*.

Oh sure...every ~~day~~ now and then I get a little emotional and tiny doubts bubble up, and I might say ~~inflammatory~~ kooky things, but I'm in total control, and there's no need for ~~another stupid~~ intervention. Calm down.

By all means, call me crazy and lock me up because I go off my my rocker once in a while after checking my email hourly only to discover that the self-appointed *Miss World* demigods have chosen not to inform me of the basics like—oh I don't know—where the #$%ing pageant is being held! Oh, and pardon me for taking a crowbar to my *Miss World* vision board (which I now have to invoice *Miss World* organizers for, unfortunately). That has *nothing* to do with menopause. It's called passion. I already said that.

Furthermore, I hardly think calling in sick ~~for a month~~ due to uncontrollable sobbing makes me depressed or—God forbid—moody! According to my life coach, uncontrollable sobbing just *might* have something to do with me putting my dreams on hold until the powers that be take a look at what they're missing! I repeat—menopause is for older women. Not me.

Plus, for your information, I can laugh too. You know what was really funny? The look on the face of the lady at Walmart who was about to grab the last package of paper towel that was on sale for $1.99 when I accidentally pressed my Peter Pointer into her back and said, "Drop it and no one gets hurt." I really needed that paper towel because I was too tired to go to another store. Pffft. I wouldn't exactly call it a hold-up, but store security had to "get involved" and remind me that humor is subjective and some people are super ~~weird~~ skittish. Blah. Blah. Blah. Honestly, some people take themselves too seriously. Sue me if it still makes me chuckle. Her face was all like—*oh my God!! Take the paper towel. Take it!* Ha! Ha!

Look, I'll be the first one to admit when menopause strikes, and, who knows, I might even write a book about it. For now, though, I'm just a girl with a dream who gets emotionally sidelined ~~every hour or so~~ once in a while. Big hairy deal. I hope when menopause does strike, I can still be passionate and keep shooting ~~myself in the foot~~ for the stars. Stay tuned, because I'm not menopausal yet. I already said that.

This 40-something Author Dates
Don Draper—Deal with It

I get the feeling people have been questioning my age. It's hardly my fault I look ~~80~~ 20. Pfft. Obviously, a true beauty queen never reveals her age, but, I will say that I recently celebrated a milestone birthday with none other than Don Draper. Still care about how old I am now? Didn't think so. Boom.

Around the time of this milestone birthday, I was super obsessed with Jon Hamm's character, Don Draper, from the hit TV show *Mad Men*. So what if I wrote him a letter or two ~~million~~. Who even cares that I bought a one-way ticket to LA and briefly camped outside his huge and awesome home—just kidding—I glamped. As *if* I'd camp. OMG, I hate camping!

Glamping turned out to be less fun than I had imagined. Get this—as I was coming out from behind the tree where I had just relieved myself, I was approached by a heavy-handed LAPD cop who got all up in my face about how stalking someone was illegal and how I was scaring the neighbours. Blah. Blah. Blah. I zipped my pants and came out swinging, "Define stalking, Mr Tough Guy! Plus, I'll have you know that in Canada people with dreams aren't viewed as hardened criminals. We glamp wherever we damn well please! Oh and by the way, since I can't even find a plug-in for my flat iron, I have zero interest in staying here a minute longer anyway. If you'll kindly give me back my binoculars, I'll be on my way!" What they say about LA is true. Everyone is super fake. Save your money.

After Phil picked me up at the airport and asked me how the 'teaching conference' went, I decided to give up on ~~life~~ Jon Hamm and his totally hot alter ego, Don Draper. His real-life voice probably isn't as smooth as Tennessee whiskey anyway. Whatever. Then—just as I was entering day thirteen of uncontrollable sobbing—something amazing happened. This mysteriously arrived at my door!!

OMG! OMG! OMG! Was this really happening?! Don Draper wanted me!! Eeeeeeee!! He must have seen me glamping and admired my gusto! It doesn't matter how it happened—what matters is I was soon going to ~~be his wife~~ meet him!! I spent the entire day getting ready for the big date—there was so much to do! I got highlights, a perky new outfit, and liposuction. Boom. Then after lunch I brought out the big guns: liver spot removal, skin tag cryotherapy, facial laser resurfacing, and buttocks injections. I was ready for *the Don*! With one last look in the mirror, I hollered to Phil, "Off to another teaching conference!!" and disappeared into the night.

As I entered the bar in which Don Draper had requested my presence, I was a total wreck. I didn't know how to act! Should I let him do all the talking? Take a selfie with him right away? Put my bra back on?? Then, before I could answer my own questions, the crowd parted and there he was—sitting with his leg crossed, smoking a Lucky Strike, and giving me his signature sultry look. I pointed to the NO SMOKING sign but Don doesn't follow rules. I shrugged and walked all sexy-like toward him. He was totally expressionless, obviously gobsmacked by my beauty. Duh. He was super entranced and silent, so I had to be the first to speak. With tears in my eyes, I whispered, "It's me, Don—*Miss Nackawic 1981*. I'm here for reals."

As I leaned in for a smooch, my so-called friends jumped out from behind him and yelled, "Surprise!! Happy birthday!!" They were dressed up as characters from *Mad Men* and they thought they were just sooo clever. ~~Idiots~~. They asked, "What do you think of Don Draper?? Is he stiff or what? Ha! Ha!" Jealous losers. What kind of friends ruin a date night with a Hollywood celeb?! OMG. I tried to forgive them for trying to steal me from my ~~cardboard~~ man, but I was seething and I just couldn't hold back, "What ~~the #$%~~ are you guys *doing* here?? I'm on a date!!"

They pretended like they didn't hear me and asked if I wanted a Manhattan (Don's drink of choice), so I skulked to the bar and pounded back ~~fourteen~~. I was gonna have to make the best of this crap night. Just wait 'til their 50ths…grrrrr. Ooops!! I didn't mean to say 50. Forget I said that, k?

With each Manhattan I ~~guzzled~~ sipped, I softened towards my friends. They were jealous as hell, but, if I were them, I would be too. I was Don Draper's date, for the *lovovgod*! Let that sink in for a minute. To be honest, I was sorta glad they showed up to wreck my date because, as gorgeous as Don is, he didn't utter a single word all night. He just stared and smoked, stared and smoked, stared and smoked all night long. I found him flat but in the end I still took him home with me. Not many people can say that, so suck it.

It turned out to be a super fun party—I still call it a date but my sabotage-happy friends refer to it as a surprise party, so I feel I should too. Whatever. At my age, I have to learn to go with the flow and deal with terrible things like a hot date turning into a drunken birthday shindig filled with presents and tons of attention. Sucks, but it's a sign of maturity. Another sign of maturity is realizing that sometimes your dream man is simply shallow and mute and that ~~rough serrated cardboard edges cause chafing~~ you have to adjust. At least he doesn't interrupt.

PS I'm done with Don.

Phil is way hotter anyway, and he actually talks ~~on Wednesdays~~. Jealous much?

Section 5

~~Not~~ Saving the World
and
~~Not~~ Developing My Talents

I'm a Giver of Life, You Guys!

Ever notice how *Miss World* contestants blab on and on about how they want to save the world? Pfft…doing what may I ask—building schools in third world countries?? Starting a new colony on Mars?? Give me a break! Those things are fine I suppose, but how many of them have had invasive procedures in the name of mankind the way I have? I have literally given of myself to save others. You heard me. I gave blood. I'm a living donor!

Being selfless is the 49th most desirable trait of a beauty queen according to *Page 17, Section B, Subsection 3C* of my handbook. Despite my deathly fear of needles, I let a stranger drive one into my arm so that others could live.

And for your information, I did *not* do it for the free juice and cookies afterwards, so you can stop tweeting about the fact that I ate an entire box of free OREOS.

On the drive to the blood clinic, I couldn't ~~avoid two squirrels and a porcupine~~ block out my childbirth memory in which the nurse tried for forty-five minutes to ram the IV into my super toned arm. "Do you even *have* a vein?!" she asked. To which I replied, "Well, if you think wearing a tiara to the delivery room is vain, then *you're* the one with problems!" It was devastating being pricked with a needle over and over, yet here I was facing my fear head on. I never knew I had such strength.

When I arrived at the donor clinic, I couldn't help but notice the decor. The entire place screamed blood—red walls, red chairs, and the red dots that I saw just before I hit the red floor. When I came to, I was asked to wear a special badge that read: ~~DO NOT RESUSCITATE~~ I'M A FIRST TIME DONOR.

Next, a nurse asked me some questions. Then she very rudely stabbed my Peter Pointer. I blurted, "Owwwwwwwww!! You're being mean to me!! That hurt like hell, but I saved a life! Book me in for three months and point me towards the cookies! Boom. Done."

Nurse Almighty got huffy and told me I had not yet given blood. WTF. Apparently, that was just a quality check to make sure I wasn't trying to kill anyone with tainted blood. Talk about paranoid. Why they wouldn't take my word that my blood was safe was beyond me. After a sixty-minute self-imposed breather, I moved on to the next stage—a questionnaire. I was appalled by some of the personal questions: *In the last twelve months have you had or been treated for syphilis or gonorrhea?* (Who wants to know??) *In the last 6 months have you handled monkeys or their bodily fluids?* (Who hasn't? Duh.) *In the last twelve months have you been in jail or prison and, if so, were you bitten by an inmate!* (So what if I was!!) I literally felt spied on.

Next, I was led to the bloodletting chair. A young nurse came towards me, examined my arm, and remarked, "Your veins are so tiny! You might be ~~dead~~ dehydrated." I fought for my life as she poked, prodded, and stabbed me trying to find a vein. A senior nurse suggested I ~~stop yelling, "Take me now!! I've had a good life!"~~ try the other arm, but she assured me I need not feel pressured to stay. I hesitated, but then I remembered the bigger picture and bravely said, "But I really want ~~those damn cookies~~ to save a life!!"

I tried to relax and remind myself how good ~~those cookies would taste~~ it would feel to *literally* save millions of lives. As I daydreamed, I realized the nurse had managed to insert the needle. She said my blood was like porridge and gave me little tips to make it flow better—squeeze my hand, wiggle my fingers, and hang ~~like a sloth from the light fixtures~~ onto positive thoughts. I floated in and out of consciousness for an hour ~~while a hot doctor dabbed my forehead with a warm cloth and told me I was the bravest, most beautiful woman he'd ever met~~ and then—boom—it was over! I got another special badge: I ~~AM BANNED~~ GAVE BLOOD. Talk about proud of myself! I was literally a saint!

It turns out the so-called experts were totally right! Not only did I save over seven million lives with my good deed, but I made some new friends when I hunkered down for my cookies afterwards. Well…not *everyone* turned out to be my friends—some of those weirdoes ratted me out, but it's only because they were mad that they got crappy Arrowroot biscuits. It's hardly my fault I'm a fast eater, and there was a sign that said, *Help yourself.* Oreos are my total faves. Oh well…I have to rise above negative people like that and focus on my purpose which—until I become *Miss World*—is obviously ~~eating cookies~~ saving the entire universe with my super awesome blood.

I Rocked the Ice Bucket Challenge!

While I waited for *Miss You Know What* to materialize, I committed to changing the world, one act of kindness at a time. The *ALS Ice Bucket Challenge* in 2014 was not something I was about to shy away from, and I was determined to raise ~~my Facebook profile~~ awareness for ALS. I didn't love the idea of someone dumping a bucket of ice over my head, but, beside hopefully finding a cure, I totally had to see if I could still rock a wet t-shirt. Not that I was in many wet t-shirt contests back in the day, but I do recall being doused with an occasional bucket of water ~~weekly~~ while I writhed on a pub table, screaming and pretending to hate it. It landed me a husband. Boom.

The organizers of the *Bucket Challenge* were clearly paranoid and had trust issues because you had to prove that you accepted and completed the challenge by posting it on Facebook. If I was going to be splashed all over ~~magazine covers~~ Facebook, I wanted to look amazingly fabulous, obviously. I hired a hair stylist, a wardrobe person, and an *Ice Bucket Challenge* consultant—someone who tells you where to stand, how to look sexy as the ice cubes cascade down your shirt, and how to edit the swear words from your video. Then, I chose a scorcher of a day so the water would refresh me and cling to my see-through tank top. Finally, I invited a photographer from *Cosmopolitan* magazine, but settled on my husband when my 600 urgent calls to the "terribly busy" magazine got forwarded to the authorities. Their loss.

On the morning of the challenge, I woke up at 10:30, totally eager to do my part to make the world a better place. My stylist arrived too early, so I asked him to sit outside on my step until I'd had my third latte. OMG, some people, right?? Once I was fully caffeinated, we got to work preparing for the video. First, my consultant presented various bucket-holding options. After we settled on pouring the bucket down my front, the sun went behind a cloud. So much for that steamy hot backdrop I was going for. We would just have to wait it out despite my camera crew of a husband becoming huffy and barking, "This is taking hours!" Wow—so selfish! It felt like he wasn't in this for the right reasons. Whatever.

After hair touch-ups and vocal coaching, it was finally show time. I looked into the camera, announced my *Ice Bucket Challenge* nomination, and sang a breathless rendition of *Happy Birthday, Mr. President.* Then I drizzled a smidge of water down my arm and fake-screamed. My consultant informed me I looked like a wannabe, so I had no choice but to give 'er. So I wouldn't fake it, I had my consultant dump the bucket over my head this time. As the ice cubes wrecked my hair, I screamed terrible obscenities and instinctively took to the grass, squirming and thrashing about like a salmon on a river bank. Old habits die hard. Sue me.

I looked up from my grassy pose to see the neighbors and our teenagers staring at me with the weirdest looks on their faces. They obviously didn't recognize the face of volunteerism and selflessness, but that wasn't about to stop me. I had single handedly raised awareness for the cause!

I dried off, went inside to make a donation to ALS, and tried to upload my video onto Facebook to prove I'd done it. I wasn't sure which button was the upload one, so I hollered to Alex and Max to come help me, but they were too busy throwing up. Honestly, I sometimes wonder if I'm in the right family—they just don't seem to think of other people the way I do.

The *Ice Bucket Challenge* was a worthy cause, and I can't get over how selfless I am! Sure, it took an entire afternoon and totally wrecked my hair, but it did prove once and for all that I can not rock a wet t-shirt and that I'm a giver. I hope that anyone reading this will take my lead and try to make the world a better place. Just don't forget to film yourself doing your good deed because, otherwise, it's like it never even happened, and what's the point of that? Duh.

I Wrote a Bo-ok! Na! Na! Na! Poo! Poo!

News flash: Not only do I fill my days with selfless giving, but I also found the time to write a children's book ~~with two coauthors~~ all by myself! Boom. It's called *Follow the Goose Butt, Camelia Airheart!* and it's about a Canada goose with no sense of direction, and no—it is *not* autobiographical, so why don't you give it a rest and stop telling everyone I can't find my way out of a paper bag!?

Here I am with ~~Odette Barr~~ a copy of the book I wrote all by myself

Fine. Be weird and super nitpicky about the details—I suppose I did have a *tiny* bit of help writing the #1 bestseller, but I still deserve the lion's share of the royalties no matter what those loophole-obsessive lawyers say! My cowriters, Odette Barr and Beth Weatherbee, (Put your glasses on if you can't see! Hardly my fault.) did contribute to the book, and, God knows, they'll never let me forget it. Read my lips: egomaniacs. Whatever. If you must know, we came up with the idea on a road trip a few years ago. Sure, it was super fun to talk about writing a book, but I had no idea they were serious, or I would have refused their help because I'm a total lone wolf when it comes to creativity. Here's how I roll once I get a juicy idea:

> *Open computer. Stare at screen. Make coffee. Drink coffee. Check Facebook. Check Twitter. Alphabetize canned goods. Make more coffee. Drink more coffee. Google 'Canada geese'. Polish tiara. Wrestle*

with ~~corkscrew~~ doubt. Stare out window. Pluck chin hair. Type any-
thing that comes to mind. e.g. 'This is so lame. Writing sucks.' Check
Pinterest. Check Facebook. Unfriend anyone who looks purposeful.
Fold clothes that have been in dryer for ~~fourteen~~ days. Stare at Miss
World vision board. Type another sentence e.g. 'Who even cares
about a dumb goose? I quit!' Turn off computer.

See what I mean? I literally couldn't imagine sharing my super intense
process with others, but, since Odette and Beth are essentially passive-aggressive
bullies, I felt I had no choice but to let them work with me on this awesome
book that I had, obviously, half written on my own already (See above).

We literally started writing the day after we got the idea. Obsessive
much? Don't say I said so, but I could tell right away that sharing my gifts
with these two was going to be the biggest mistake of my life. Get this—we
had done literally nothing but write and discuss ideas for twelve non-stop
minutes when I realized we hadn't taken a break yet. You heard me. When
I *dared* to suggest I needed a ~~nap~~ snack and another latte, you'd swear I'd
asked to be their sole beneficiaries—which I did ask later, by the way, and it
went over like a lead balloon. Slave drivers *and* financially paranoid. Wow.

We eventually got into a rhythm, and it became clear that each of us had
something to bring to the writing table, especially me. Beth thinks we'll get
Camelia Airheart on TV, even though *I'm* the one who's a natural in front
of the camera. She also sings, so she wrote and then recorded the music for
the *Branta Bog Ballad* for our book. Big whoop. Odette is logical and practical
and tells us we have to write it before it can become a TV show and that *no*
we can't finish this book *and* write a sitcom by the end of the day and be
famous by Monday. ~~No one likes her.~~ Plus, she's the big shot illustrator, even
though I submitted goose drawings for the book, but she said, "Ha! Ha!
These are hilarious!"

Pfft. Who even cares? I have talents too obviously. I make a mean latte with the perfect frothed milk/coffee ratio; I wear fashionable ~~sweatpants~~ clothes to our writing sessions; and I become super enraged when they use too many adverbs. I'm a wordsmith whom 'the others' have dubbed Semi-Colleen (because I love semi-colons obviously) which doesn't bother me as much as they hoped it would, so there! I'm also super picky about word choice. The following sentence took three hours to write and shows how seriously I take this. Writing is hard.

~~A The An A The An Several Many~~ One ~~small tiny little, large, super awesome duck~~ gigantic goose ~~flew hurled skittered, soared~~ raced ~~over above, through~~ across ~~a an~~ the ~~sky horizon~~ atmosphere.

By the end of that first writing session it became clear they needed me to make good ~~lattes~~ word choices. Even though I always imagined myself in the limelight totally alone, I decided to stick with them for a few more books in the Camelia Airheart series. It's for their sake, not mine. I could easily write a book and become super famous without a lick of help, but it wouldn't be ~~illustrated or coherent~~ the same without them I suppose. Whatever.

PS I perform the book with various facial expressions and voices, and I seriously think this will separate me from the other *Miss World* contestants who perform dumb gymnastic routines and sing boring opera songs. Grow up!

Bye Bye Privacy and Normal Life!

Don't get me wrong—I'd totally love to take a selfie right now and send it to you but MY EYES ARE BLOODSHOT FROM THE ~~PRE-TEND~~ PAPARAZZI'S CAMERA FLASHES! I ~~love~~ hate to brag, but ~~our~~ my book is in *Chapters*! You heard me. Hold your applause—I just need a little break from all the attention. Okay. Break's over. You can clap again.

Seriously though—be careful what you wish for. I used to look at famous authors and think ~~their books suck~~ how awesome it would be to have my face splashed all over Chapters' bookshelves like that. Then it happened to me, and I couldn't have been less prepared for the aftermath. It was totally ~~non-existent~~ ugly. This is a cautionary tale, obviously.

After ~~our~~ my book, *Follow the Goose Butt, Camelia Airheart!* was released, I literally couldn't contain myself. I drove ~~100 km/h~~ to the most famous book store in the universe to see ~~our~~ my #1 bestseller. As I pulled into the parking lot, my excitement turned to total darkness. All of a sudden it hit me—I was a celeb, and I could no longer just waltz into public places like regular, unpublished people. I'd be mobbed for sure! Bye, bye privacy and normal life! I parked the car and sat there for a minute, wondering how Oprah handled this fishbowl existence. The parking lot was empty, thank God, so I slithered in on my stomach like a snake. No one noticed except the weird little kid who pointed at me and said, "Mommy! The snake lady is scaring me!" Boo! Hoo! Note to parents: Quit protecting your kids from the real world and teach a little tolerance. Good Lord.

Once inside Chapters (the most famous book store in the universe), I shielded my eyes and squinted hard, awaiting the literal frenzy of the ~~non-existent~~ camera flashes. After smashing into a wall by mistake, I opted instead for a disguise so I wouldn't have to walk around squinting, which is not a good look for me. I grabbed a scarf off the shelf and wrapped it around my head so fast that I didn't even realize it wasn't my color!! I know, right?! I looked totally washed out, but it was the price I had to pay for instant fame.

Next, I whipped out my massive, Hollywood-like sunglasses and covered my eyes. I found a copy of ~~our~~ my book and hid behind a bookshelf. Suddenly I had deep empathy for Justin Bieber and felt his pain. I also felt my pain because I got a super terrible cramp in my foot while I was crouching. Then I thought I heard someone call ~~security~~ "OMG it's J. Lo!" I prayed I'd be able to outrun the paparazzi when the time came.

Pfft. I must have been hearing things because no one chased me. Weirdest store ever! I came out from hiding and roamed around incognito for a while, and I couldn't believe how many places I found the book. This thing was on total FI-YAH! Check it.

It was in the travel section because Camelia, the Canada goose, travels all across New Brunswick. Duh.

It's only been in the store for an hour and this happened! Hashtag blessed!

When did the staff even have time to read it? Boom.

Even the CEO of Chapters chose ~~us~~ me!!

Here's the shelf most of them are on. I find it unfair that the other authors don't have a fighting chance but the store manager must have wanted the books displayed this way.

Aaaaaand here's a close -up of the book:

No I'm *not* hiding two other names! FYI, I got plenty of attention as a child and I'd hardly call taking my parents' car for a joyride when I was ten attention-seeking. I'd call it gutsy, so deal with it. PS I just unfriended you on Facebook.

The crowds were a little ~~invisible~~ thin because it was supper time, so I decided to remove the scarf and sunglasses, and let the ~~imaginary~~ fans have a shot at meeting me. As I slipped the sunglasses back into my purse, I heard the words I'd waited my entire life to hear, "Would you mind signing these?" One of the employees had figured out I was the ~~co~~author from when I jumped out of hiding and screamed, "Hey guess what everyone!?? I wrote this book all by myself!!" and asked me to sign a few copies. Then she put this sticker on it: Signed by the AUTHOR—Note the singular noun. Boom.

The signing went on for ~~seconds~~ hours. My wrist was practically falling off, but it was totally worth it!!

As the lights dimmed and the manager said, "~~For the last time, we're~~

~~closing! Go home, diva!~~ Closing time." I glanced around the empty store one last time. Apparently, security guards are very impatient people because halfway through my thank you speech, he rolled his eyes and turned off all the lights!! ~~Idiot~~. Anyway, the experience was a total ~~bust~~ rush! Don't be jealous. You have no idea what it's like to hide from the paparazzi and wear colours that wash you out—it's a special kind of hell only the famous can experience, but I suppose I'm going to have to get used to it once I'm *Miss World*, right??

PS I'm not allowed within twenty feet of Chapters for a 'trial period' (Blah. Blah. Blah.), but if you would like me to sign your book, call my ~~pretend~~ agent and we can arrange it at an awesome independent bookstore instead. Air kiss. Boom.

Chapters. Schmapters. Pfft

Chapter, Schmapters. Pfft. Guess what?? I thought ~~we~~ I was super famous when ~~our~~ my book was in Chapters, but something even better happened to catapult ~~us~~ me into the stratosphere of total famedom. ~~We~~ I got invited to speak at a children's literature conference with other famous authors!! Obviously, it's only a matter of time before I have my own bodyguard, clothing line, and Smoky Cat Eye make-up expert. Boom.

Who even cares if ~~we were~~ I was the warm-up act for the keynote speakers who would hog the limelight the next day. Whatever. After ~~our~~ my awesome presentation, it was time to cash in on my ~~free drink~~ newfound celebrity status and hobnob with the prestigious authors who didn't even know I was ~~Miss Nackawic 1981~~ also a writer. I was too tired to sign autographs anyway.

The next morning, we had to 'support' the ~~show-off~~ authors who apparently commanded a crowd. Pfft. I hardly even noticed that it was standing room only as people piled in for the keynote speakers. Big deal. The introductions went on and on and were laced with words like: *prolific, award-winning,* and *renowned*. Blah. Blah. Blah.

The first presenter dazzled us with her ~~overrated~~ illustrations. She creates art and writes stories and she must have said that—like—fifteen million times. We get it!! Cripes. As she showed the audience photographs of her artwork at various stages, I could hardly hear myself think from all the "Ooohs" and "Ahhhs". Frig. "Anyone can do that!" I thought to myself. To prove it, once home, I went straight to Walmart and dropped $1.99 on some modelling clay and got to work, creating our main character, Camelia Airheart, the Canada goose:

Boom. ~~Mutilated~~ Nailed it.

I'll bet she feels silly spending all that time on her art after seeing what ~~delusional~~ inexperienced people can do with clay.

Next on the roster of ~~show-offs~~ established children's authors was one who writes picture books, chapter books, non-fiction books, and novels. She writes approximately a book/hour and each one of them is nominated for an award. Big whoop. Pardon me if I can't write every minute of the day because that would leave me zero time for Netflix. Frig that.

The next presenter had too much talent for her own good. In hindsight, I probably shouldn't have hollered, "Get off the stage!!" in the middle of her presentation, but it just got my goat that she had it all. She's a children's author and a renowned artist and a sculptor who creates teensy weensy sculptures from fine Japanese papers, and her work has been displayed in galleries around the world. She even sold a paper sculpture to Ben Stiller!! (Oh yea?! Well, I won the Easter bunny drawing contest at my school in Grade 3, so there!) Her paper sculptures were cool, but I wondered why she spends so much time on these ~~stupid~~ tiny sculptures when I could make one in under five minutes.

Ta da! I call this one *Piece of ~~Crap~~ Snow,* and Ben Stiller is likely in a bidding war for it on eBay at this very moment. Hmmph.

The pièce de résistance and final author of the weekend has made a big time name for herself, and let's just say the ~~loud, crybabies~~ kids that showed up to hear her read practically trampled me down to get to her. Babies were sliding out of their mothers' wombs weeks early just to hear her read for crissakes. Miss Show-Off of the Century held the ~~annoying~~ kids rapt with her tongue twisters that she had memorized. While she read, I wondered how hard it would be to write that stuff as I rubbed my soft 'bankie' against my nose and sucked my thumb. During coffee break, I scratched out my very own tongue twister on a napkin. Newsflash: It was effortless!! Check it:

Um… I hate to brag but that took me like–two nanoseconds.

It was a totally amazing weekend! I learned how easy it is to do the things that these authors/artists spend ridiculous amounts of time supposedly perfecting. I just don't get why people don't chill and watch more Netflix. Duh. Look at ~~us~~ me—I'm super famous and I've only written one book. But I'm also *Miss Nackawic 1981* though, and not a lot of people have that claim to fame.

I Just Came off a Gruelling Promo Tour, You Guys!

~~We~~ I just came off a gruelling promotional tour. You heard me—tour. ~~Odette, Beth and~~ I participated in the totally coveted, one and only literary festival—the *2017 Frye Fest* during which ~~we~~ I ~~rocked out~~ read from ~~our~~ my super famous book, *Follow the Goose Butt, Camelia Airheart!* I know you're jealous, but, being on the road for ~~two days~~ half your life isn't as glamorous as it looks. Fame can be gut-wrenching and thankless, and, in my darkest moments, I admit it—I longed for my old life back. True story.

When I stepped out of the ~~car~~ limo after arriving at the first gig, I knew my life would never be the same. I took a deep breath before being ushered into the ~~smoky venue~~ public library. I was handed tour swag in the form of a badge with unlimited access to all Frye Festival events, a schedule for the week, and, as per my demand, a family-sized bag of red only (absolutely no peanuts!) M&Ms in straight rows of 10. Boom. Famous.

It was show time. The kids were like friggin' groupies—they were screaming and rolling around on the floor like rabid animals. The tension was insane, and you could literally feel the building shake. In a frenzy, I grabbed the mic and screamed, "Hello, Monctoonnn!! ~~Miss Nackawic 1981 is in the hoouussse!!~~ Are you ready to ~~rock~~ read??!" The fans were out of their minds! They laughed, they cried, and some even wet themselves! This was hard-core. At the end of it, I had to barricade myself as the crowd ran toward ~~the stupid snack table~~ me for an autograph. It was a total rush, but also a bit scary because security was nowhere in sight. I could have been killed.

No clue who those three are but
obviously I've been Photobombed.
Grrrr.

Here's me in the limelight, exactly the way God intended:

Do not try this at home. This is after hours and hours in the make-up chair while I sipped lattes and screamed, "You *know* I don't look good in earth tones, and I don't care if I have sparse eyebrows, grey roots, a burgeoning beard or chapped lips—that's your problem to fix. Not mine."

The next tour stop was filled with highly demanding toddlers. These guys had literally zero appreciation for the arts or what it's like to be on the road day after friggin' day. They didn't give a tinker's damn that my throat had a tickle and I had to scream over them while they babbled, danced, and drank non-stop from their sippy cups. Grow up!! It was a regular ~~mosh pit~~ daycare. Those were the hardest thirty minutes of the tour, obviously.

After ~~two~~ endless days of press junkets, the thrill of the tour was starting to wear off, but I didn't for one second consider quitting. ~~Our~~ My contract was super clear—I had to show up at each event regardless of my mental state. The show must go on! At the next leg of the tour, I was greeted by an eight-year-old girl who took one look at my oversized sunglasses and blonde wig disguise and whispered, "Are you ~~Miss Nackawic 1981~~ the author?" I was like, "Duh." She showed ~~us~~ me to the classroom where we would be performing for star-struck ~~groupies~~ Grade 3 students. At this point, I didn't even know which city I was in—hand to God—so it shocked everyone when I grabbed the mic and yelled, "Hello, Montreal!! Let's ~~rock~~ read like yo' Mama taught you!!!" By the end of the performance ~~we~~ I had them in the palm of my hand. They totally loved ~~us~~ me which made the exhaustion, dehydration, and chronic throat tickle almost worth it.

The post-reading autograph signing was civilized for a change, which allowed for a few questions from the crowd: *Can you sign my ~~bicep~~ lunchbox? Do you know ~~Justin Bieber~~ my cousin who goes to your school? His name is Forest and he has brown hair. Are you ~~wearing a wig~~ famous?*

Time restraints only allowed for one photo-op...~~which was taken by the teacher on her iPhone~~. As the last ~~wisp of dry ice vanished~~ bell rang for the day, I knew it was my cue to hit the road again. Would they remember me tomorrow? Would my signature on their ~~biceps~~ lunchboxes fade? Try grappling with questions like that at night, and then let me know if you still wish you were me...

I could go on and on, but the truth is every city is the same. Every stage is the same. Every adoring fan? The bloody same. The second I closed the ~~car~~ limo door at the end of that last performance, I felt empty, gutted, and lonely. It's the part of fame no one talks about—I call it the underbelly. By the end of that tour, I needed my bed, I needed my space, but mostly I needed my beloved ~~Netflix~~ family. Don't freak out. I'll tour again. It's in my blood. For now though, I just want my old life back. I want to go to the grocery store without getting mobbed, so if you see me there, please don't approach me unless I'm waving my *Autograph Signing from 1-3* sign. Note: These rules will apply once I take the title of *Miss World*, obviously. Air kiss and peace out.

Do These Pants Make Me Look Fat? Be Honest

Not only am I amazing at folding clothes, picking up wet towels and unloading the dishwasher, but I'm also awesome at shopping for things I look hot in, and cars are no exception. When Phil told me we needed a new car, I didn't trust that he would choose something that would look good in a parade, so I tagged along. I'll have you know I also asked totally intelligent questions about mileage, safety ratings, and the lipstick mirror thingy.

After a few weeks of searching, we had narrowed our selection down to two cars. Phil insisted on visiting the car lot ~~hourly~~ daily. While he longingly caressed the ~~saleswoman~~ high-tech gadgets in the latest models, I kept us grounded by asking some awesome and smart questions:

Would an extra foam Venti cappuccino fit in those cup holders?

Where's the 8-track tape slot?

Here's Phil totally amazed with this dumb key thingy while I'm still searching for the ~~#$%ing~~ 8-track tape slot!

My husband fell in love with the fully loaded Lincoln we were eyeing. I admit it was an awesome car, but I noticed that things had changed big time since the last car we had purchased twelve years ago. That one was also fully loaded—it had roll-down windows, brakes, and a steering wheel. The Lincoln had a push-button start, park-assist camera, and ~~landing gear~~ heated seats!! It felt like being in a spaceship and pardon me for wanting to see if my coffee would really float in space! It's not like the seats weren't leather. Pfft. Everything seemed so complicated, and I suggested we just keep our

2003 ~~horse and buggy~~ Corolla. Phil panicked at the thought of not getting a new car and suggested I get ~~lost~~ familiar with the gadgets.

I slid into the driver's seat, and he activated the heated, vibrating seats ~~for three hours~~. Next, I tried to insert my *Bat Out of Hell* 8-track into the navigation system. *Note to manufacturers*: The touch screen scratches **very** easily. Holy frig.

My husband, meanwhile, was all over the ~~saleswoman~~ voice-recognition technology and said, "Check this out, honey. You can ask it questions! Try it." It's totally awkward asking a robot personal questions, but I gave it a shot and asked, "Do these pants make me look fat? Be honest." The stupid VRT robot replied, "Sorry. I didn't understand the question. Please say something else." Good Lord! I thought this was a 'smart' vehicle. I tried again, "Should I lose weight??" VRT: "Did you say you want to go to Kuwait?" *Someone* was dodging my fat questions. Wow.

After the nine-hour tutorial given by the saleswoman, I learned how to start it, program my favorite radio station, and apply a perfect Smoky Cat Eye in the lipstick mirror thingy. Finally… it was time for a test drive. Woot!! We took it for a spin ~~down to the Hamptons for the weekend~~ downtown. I drove obviously. While merging into traffic, I mistook the flashing yellow light of the side mirror sensor for a camera flash and took a *driving selfie* (of course it's a thing! Google it, haters!). This resulted in a raised finger from the driver in the passing lane. *Excuse me* for always being ready for a photo shoot, Mr. Perfect Driver!! OMG.

Guess what?? We totally bought the car and it's all because of me and my car-shopping talent! I was part of the process and my super intelligent questions really showed Phil how ~~useless~~ valuable I can be. What an awesome feeling!!! The bad news is that passive/aggressive Voice Recognition Technology/Rude Robot forced me to go home and take a good look at myself in the full-length hall mirror and get this—my pants **do** make me look fat!! Dieting sucks so that's out of the question. Oh well—I'll just look hot from the neck up. I may have to lose a few pounds for the *Miss World* float because I'll be really exposed in parades, but I'll worry about that when I win. Boom.

Section 6

I'm ~~Not~~ Extremely Athletic
and
Totally ~~Not~~ Ready
for the Bikini Portion of the Pageant—
duh

I'm ~~not~~ a Body Pump Expert

At first I refused to be body-shamed by that stupid, rude Voice Recognition Technology system in our new car, and I just continued enjoying my seven lattes (with whole milk and chocolate sprinkles) per day and learned to love my ~~sweatpants~~ body, thank you very much. I was fine with having only my upper body parade-float ready, but then something terrible happened—my arms became super friendly and continued to flap and wave long after my hand stopped. WTF! How could I wave to the little people in parade floats if my triceps had no 'off' switch?? I knew in my heart of hearts that ~~exercise~~ plastic surgery was out of the question because last time I checked it wasn't covered by my total rip-off of a health care plan! ~~Idiots.~~ I knew I had to do something if I wanted my *Miss World* evening gown to be sleeveless. Which I did, obviously.

When I didn't hear back from the thirty-seven letters I wrote to my cheapskate, bare-bones insurance company, my childhood bestie told me about a non-surgical solution—a workout called ~~Euthenasia~~ Body Pump. It started at 6 a.m. which is when I'm still sleeping, so obviously I said, "Nah. Count me out," and started a *GoFundMe* campaign for my plastic surgery. That was immediately taken down by some huffy Interweb watchdog weirdo, so I had no choice but to get buff the old-fashioned way even though it didn't sound easy or fun.

When we reached the studio at 5:45 a.m., my friend shook me awake and rudely dragged me from the ~~trunk where I was hiding~~ fetal position. I wiped the drool from my chin and shuffled to the front desk where I engaged in light conversation with the twelve-year-old, eye-rolling summer student who turned out to be super paranoid. Every question I asked her, she was like—*This isn't Starbucks, ma'am. Please stop accusing me of hiding the espresso maker.* OMG, how *dare* she call me ma'am?? How dare she! As if that wasn't insulting enough, she then forced me to sign a form which essentially absolved the studio of any responsibility in the event of a workout-related death. I almost backed out when I read Clause 92-B3, which stated that any Lululemon pants worn by the deceased will become studio property. Psych!! I had on my faded pants with holes in the crotch anyway.

Go ahead. Take 'em!!

I climbed the stairs to the ~~morgue~~ Body Pump room where my friendly, jiggly arms waved 'hello' to all their new friends while I gathered some weights, a mat, and ~~rosary beads~~ a towel in case I perspired—as if. The instructor was totally ripped and apparently killed ~~baby kittens with her bare hands~~ it in Iron Man competitions. Big hairy deal—what a show-off! Don't say I said so, but I found her arms to be very unfriendly. She singled me out as the newbie and told me to challenge myself, but go light on the weights. I assured her that I would ~~sue her ass if I broke so much as a nail, never mind into a sweat~~ be just fine thank you very much.

The class began pleasantly enough. The instructor put on some dance tunes and ~~I danced like no one was watching~~ told us to put 5-pound weights on our bars. Then she asked us to **lift** the bar containing the weights. Ha! Ha! Good one! That's when I gave up and took the opportunity to reapply my strawberry-flavored super shiny lip gloss. Ms. Navy Seals from Hell didn't approve. She gave me a death stare, but I wasn't afraid of her, and I took my sweet old time making sure to dot my lower lip with extra gloss for the pouty look before I picked up my stupid bar containing the ridiculous amount of weight.

After the first song, I prayed for a quick death. Then I heard the instructor say the most wonderful words in the entire world, "Time for lunch" I screamed, "Finally!! Praise the Lord! Club sandwich with fries and gravy for me! Woot!" and headed for the door. Then I heard Ms. Navy Seals from Hell, who clearly needs work on enunciation, bark, "I said **lunges,** not lunch!" Frig that. I ripped open the granola bar I found tucked inside my bra and gulped it down without even chewing it properly— that's how rushed I felt. OMG.

With chocolate smears all over my face, I rejoined the group, trying not to ~~kick~~ hate the mannequin women who doubled the weights on their bars. I ~~don't~~ regret tripping them by mistake when they walked by. The more weight I removed from my bar, the more they ~~pointed at me and said "75 lbs is the new obese"~~ piled onto theirs. By the end of the class, I was lifting the broom handle I found in the closet and hoping to God I ~~didn't chip a nail~~ lived to tell about it.

Right after I screamed, "Someone help me! I can't feel my arms! I'm literally crippled and my lip gloss has worn completely off!!" the music stopped, and it was over. I asked my friend to reapply my gloss before the paramedics arrived because of the mouth-to-mouth I would probably require on account of the fact that I was lying motionless on the floor. Not many people get mouth-to-mouth and an ambulance ride under their belts by 7 a.m. Don't be jealous. You probably have productive days too.

It would have been super awesome to get flowers while I was recovering from my devastating work-out experience, but I didn't put it on Facebook because my hair was flat, so how would people have known? If however, you have any lingering guilt from ignoring me in my time of need, my *GoFundMe* page could sure use some traffic. Every little bit helps especially one hundred dollar donations. Plastic surgery doesn't pay for itself and without it I can't wear a strapless gown so...

Olympic ~~Nightmares~~ Dreams

As a kid, I dreamt of being an Olympic medalist, and every Olympic Games, I am filled with horrible regret as I watch the ~~show-off~~ dedicated athletes with gleaming medals hanging from their necks. My passion for glory was unstoppable, and I tried literally every sport, but I must have lacked ~~talent, focus, and training~~ something because it didn't work out for me. After the last Olympic Games, I've come to the conclusion that, apparently, there are foolproof and weirdly obsessive and rigid ways to become an Olympian. I would have loved this information as a kid, and I'd literally be dripping in medals if I'd known!! It breaks my heart to see young athletes making the same mistakes I did—it is for them that I selflessly wrote this public service announcement for future champs. You're welcome.

☻ **Consume nutrients.** I ate Cheetos for lunch because I thought they were baby carrots, that's why, Ms Nutritionist of the Year! It's important to eat real carrots, according to Olympians.

☻ **Put in the hours.** Due to my busy schedule, I wasn't able to devote the required hours to my Olympic training. My days were already chock-a-block full with soap-opera-watching, sleeping and smoking Export As. Athletes must carve out more than 10-15 minutes/day to train.

☻ **Develop a team mentality.** Our school colors were burgundy and gold, and I didn't look good in them, so I didn't bother trying out for any teams even though the coach begged me to ~~stay away~~. Looking back, I may have overreacted. I Googled it and true athletes don't even consider the colour of the uniforms they have to wear. Imagine.

☻ **Be professional.** Apparently, you have to look like a nun to be on a swim team, and no one told me a G-string bikini was not an acceptable bathing suit option. Bye bye ~~hot swim coach~~ Olympic swimmer dream. Kids, go buy yourselves a wet suit because you'll be disqualified if you show a smidgeon of flesh. Unreal.

☻ **Listen to your coach.** My figure skating coach never let up on me because she wanted me to be ~~dead~~ the best: "Stand taller! Stop whining! For the last time, tie those #$%ing laces!!" After the third concussion from tripping on them, I quit. I had to preserve what was left of my super fragile ~~brain~~ dignity.

☺ **Be flexible**. I couldn't continue with figure skating lessons because they were offered at 8 a.m. on Saturday mornings, and I was still asleep during that time. (You try getting up at that hour after partying all night and see how much you like it.) After the eighth missed lesson, I was asked to ~~stay home~~ reconsider figure skating. Take it from me—you can't win the Olympics if you don't go to lessons because I guess that's where you learn things about your sport. I did not know this back then.

☺ **Have a mantra**. Mental fitness is half the battle. When you're discouraged and weary, repeat a self-affirming mantra that fuels your soul. Mine was, "I'm going to ~~Dairy Queen~~ the Olympics!" Feel free to steal my mantra.

☺ **Remain gracious in tough times.** Depositing dead rabbits on the front steps of coaches who cut you from teams or, worse, demanded you show up for practice, never works. It's better to take the ~~air out of their car tires~~ high road apparently. Didn't get that memo.

If I'd had this secret list of obscure tips when I was athletically inclined and could touch my toes without screaming in pain, things obviously would have turned out differently for me. Whatever. I can still rock a G-string bikini ~~in a dark cave~~, not that it's any of your business. Plus, I'm *Miss Nackawic 1981.* You can't have everything I guess.

Of Course Miss Nackawic 1981 is ~~Not~~ a Super Awesome Skier— Duh

Body Pump isn't the only way to stay in shape. Duh. For your information, *Miss Nackawic 1981* is also a ~~fair-weather~~ wicked awesome downhill skier. Boom. Recently, I dusted off my 15-year-old downhill skis and drove seven hours to a ski hill in Quebec—well, Phil drove while I snacked, slept, and screamed when he tailgated—to prove my rock solid commitment to the sport. You heard me. Then we arrived at the ski hill, and I started having second thoughts. Get this—the parking lot attendant refused to accept my MN1981 parking pass, and our ski lift tickets cost more than two plane tickets to Bora Bora! Plus the ski lodge was plastered with *Stay Alive. Wear a Helmet* posters. How was I going to get a helmet on over my tiara?!

Once I got on the chair lift and took a ~~swig of Fireball~~ look at the pretty scenery, I felt better. I ~~drank a lot~~ gushed, "Just look at this view! That sun! My new psychedelic goggles!!" During the 10-minute ride up the hill, I reminded Phil how much I loved skiing. I was all, "This is amaaazing! I can't wait to tear down that bunny hill! I am totally ~~drunk~~ one with the universe!" Boom.

When we got to the top, I remembered my fear of heights, speed, and death by height and speed. As Phil glided towards a sign with super scary hill names like *Death Do Us Part* and *Nice Knowin' Ya!,* I screamed, "Where the #$% are you going?? I'm not skiing down a black diamond run!! Are you trying to kill me for the insurance money?? Say it out loud. Say it to my face, so you can watch the life drain right out of me, you greedy son of a—" After he ~~administered CPR~~ assured me we would stick to intermediate hills, I simmered right down.

What was I so afraid of?? Holy—I totally nailed my first bunny hill run! I was in the zone, with the sun on my face and the sound of my skis carving through the snow (like in the Olympics—*that* sound) as I out-skied the lazy toddlers. When I reached my man he said, "You're doing great, honey, but remember what I told you about your poles. They are not wings. The pointy part goes in the ground, it doesn't flap at your side. We've been over this." *Someone* was obviously jealous of my new psychedelic goggles and was lashing out. Classic.

With each hill I totally aced, I became more euphoric, and I just had to share it with the world. I tweeted—*Meet 'n' Greet in lodge 6-9 pm #Miss #Nackawic #1981*; I posted on Facebook—*My beloved and I having the time of our lives on super ~~beginner~~ expert runs* and I even resorted to screaming from a mountaintop—*Hey everyone!! I'm offering free autographs and ski lessons. Step right up!!* By the end of the day, I was 'this close' to becoming a member of the ski patrol—they approached me more than once to ask me to ~~lower my poles before I took out someone's eye~~ join, but I politely declined. Too busy.

On the drive back to our adorable boutique hotel after our super fantabulous day, just for fun I prepared a PowerPoint presentation on the value of a ski vacation—last count I had 52 bullet points. Boom. Once at the hotel, I kept my ski boots on and clunked down to the bar where I exclaimed to no one in particular, "What a day!! Just fantastic! The slopes were wicked awesome! Can't wait for the ~~bartender to take my order~~ next ski day!!"

The next day something terrible happened—I woke up in total pain, unable to move and screamed, "I need a chiropractor, STAT!! I can't walk! I'm literally crippled!!" Phil, who pretends he's deaf half the time anyway, said, "Let's go so we can get to the hill when it opens." I replied, "Are you on actual full-blown crack?? Do you want me dead?? My muscles have seized up, and there is freezing drizzle in the forecast!! We can't ski today!"

We drove to the stupid ski hill in silence except for the weird crackling sound my computer made when I set the PowerPoint presentation on fire. We were silent on the chair lift too—Phil no doubt was plotting how to 'off me' on the first run. Pfft. I became super ~~certifiable~~ chatty, however, as I skied down the hill: "My legs!!! Abort!! Abort!! I can't do this!! Airlift me out of here!! Don't let my perfect form fool you! I'm literally dying!!" *Mr. Insurance Money* stayed like seventeen miles ahead of me for whatever reason. See if I care.

I knew ~~our marriage~~ I was in trouble when he noticed there was no line-up at the T-Bar ski lift and said, "Let's go up on the T-bar, less crowded." I responded, "I hope you ~~remarry one day~~ know my legs will literally snap off my hips if I have to stand against this metal bar for twenty minutes!! Why do you hate me all of a sudden??" He had the nerve to question my commitment to sport, "Yesterday you loved skiing. What changed?" to which I responded, "*Yesterday*??! Are you kidding me?? *Yesterday* the sun was shining, and I wasn't crippled, and the ski patrol couldn't get enough of me, and I was ~~drunk~~ happy, and the conditions were better, and I didn't realize there was a cute little bistro across the street from our hotel where I should be right now sipping a latte and practising my French!!" Sometimes I wonder if we even speak the same language. OMG.

On the drive home, I patted myself on the back for my rock solid commitment to sport. Not one to rest on my laurels I then blurted out my best idea yet, "I'm thinking we'll go somewhere warm next year. I need a new talent for the pageant—I think I'll be an Olympian surfer ~~for one hour~~. Boom."

~~Unfortunately,~~ I Can't Cook for a Month
Because I Got Hit by a Car

Recently, my cycling career literally caused me to stare death in the eye!!
I came 'this close' to being the victim of vehicular manslaughter. Oh yes you
can die from getting hit by a car that comes to a rolling stop! I'm lucky to
be alive even though it feels like no one takes me seriously at times. I came
'this close' to not having a future ~~as Miss World~~!! Warning: Graphic details.
Reader discretion is advised.

It started like any regular day. After downing my breakfast of champi-
ons—bacon and eggs and waffles and Sugar Crisp—my ~~muffin top bulged
over~~ six-pack abs were tucked into my super tight stretchy biker shorts that
I wear around the house in case I decide to go biking one day. Well, that day
happened and I have ~~self diagnosed~~ PTSD to show for it!

I had no idea what was in store for me as I dug for my bike in the garage
underneath our winter tires and Christmas decorations. I was ready for ~~a
nap~~ the ride of my life, and I was hell-bent on beating my personal best of
10 km in ~~260~~ minutes! Boom. The Tour-de-France-like trail began with a 5-
km stretch through the woods. I had just emerged from the first leg of the
totally ~~flat~~ hilly trail and stopped briefly to ~~vomit~~ catch my breath before I
bravely biked onto the city streets to finish the remaining half of the trail.

As I approached a small street at ~~turtle~~ lightning speed, I caught a
glimpse of a blue car coming down the street towards the stop sign. I slowed
down, but something terrible happened—the driver didn't even slow down
or stop at the stop sign. The homicidal sociopath behind the wheel didn't
see me, mainly because she just didn't look! Who in God's name doesn't
notice the sun glaring off a jewelled tiara??

This next part gets pretty graphic, so I'll ~~never~~ forgive you if you can't get
through it. I felt the side of the car push me to the ground. You heard me.
After free-falling for ~~two seconds~~ what felt like hours, I landed ankle-first
on the hot asphalt, breaking my death spiral with my hands and wrecking
two newly polished nails in the process. Feel guilty for judging me now??

I lay there, a crumpled shell of my former awesome self, praying that my tiara wasn't wrecked and that I would survive this terrifying incident. My bike was on top of me. I was super dizzy and disoriented, but I came out of my stupor when I saw blood ~~trickling~~ gushing down my leg! I panicked. How would I ever carry out my ~~Miss World~~ motherly duties with a missing leg??

What do you *mean* you can't see it? Please go immediately to an optometrothologist because you are obviously blind.

I yelled, "I need a blood transfusion, stat!!!" but apparently you have to be in a 'sterilized' environment for that, which is code for no one really gave a crap that I was bleeding out. Whatever.

The homicidal driver finally decided to get out of her car, probably to finish me off. She looked all of twelve years old. She ran towards me with her hand over her mouth and yelled, "OMG, are you ~~Miss Nackawic 1981~~ okay???"

I couldn't even answer. The extent of my injuries had sunk in. I totally lost it and screamed, "Tell my family I love them, and it has been an honour to be an awesome wife and mother to them. If I survive this, tell them I literally won't be able to cook for at least a month!" I was weak and slurring my words. I feared ~~another~~ brain injury. In my confusion, I went into auto-pilot and started signing autographs for the rubbernecks circling the crash site. Honestly I don't know why I bothered because they didn't have a clue where Nackawic was, much less who reigned over the town for 365 days in 1981, during which time I was under such scrutiny that I literally felt like I was living in a fishbowl!! Live under a rock much? Cripes.

Autograph-signing is like smelling salts to a beauty queen, and 'just like that' I was back to my old self. My maternal instincts took over, and I found myself gently scolding the young driver: "Do you even know how to read the word STOP, you moron?? What were you thinking? Oh wait. Never mind. People without brains can't think!!! For your information, I was having an amazing hair day until this helmet, which is hard to adjust over my tiara by the way, slid to the side in my fall—thanks to your rolling stop that caused me to land on the ground in a pool of blood!" She swore she had learned her lesson and that my hair still looked super fab, so I decided not to sue her, mainly because of the second thing she said.

Somehow I managed to stop the bleeding and bravely biked all the way home. As soon as I got through the door, I called my husband to tell him how lucky I was to ~~not have to cook for a month~~ be alive! He was breathless with questions, "Uh. Who *is* this?" ~~Idiot.~~

Recovery was slow. The ~~pretend~~ doctor told me I was a ~~hypochondriac~~ very brave woman. I fought him tooth and nail to continue my regular duties, but he said I absolutely must stay off my injured leg, lest I compromise the healing process. I just couldn't risk it.

Which is why this is happening:

Here's me looking at the clock wishing like hell I could prepare something— anything!!—for my menfolk for supper! What a total drag, right? Frig.

So the obvious moral of this story is to be super careful, always wear ~~makeup~~ a helmet, and don't trust drivers to ~~recognize a celeb when they see one~~ look both ways! Sometimes I can't believe the risks I take in the name of *Miss World.* Maybe I should re-evaluate this whole thing and protect what matters—my life! Psych!!! Ha! Ha! Never.

I'm ~~Not~~ a Total Yogi

Good posture is of utmost importance in the pageant world. I should know—I won one in 1981. After hunching over my vision board for a few decades, I noticed my shoulders had rounded. Even though I still had great hair and a winning personality ~~disorder~~, I knew I had to improve my posture if I wanted to go all the way to the top. To help me achieve a pageant-worthy stance, I signed up for yoga.

When I arrived for my first class, I couldn't help but notice my yogi was super toned, flexible and young. I hated to have to blurt out, "You've got a massive spinach leaf between your front teeth!!" in the middle of class ~~even though she didn't~~, but I wanted her to know I had her ~~stupid, fat-free~~ back.

Oh sure, she could balance all her ninety-six pounds on her pinkie, but I wasn't one bit intimidated by her. Why should I be? I could do amazing things too, and we had so much in common it was unreal:

🙂 We both had a head. Boom.

🙂 We both paid two million dollars for our sustainable, non-toxic, organic, non-flammable, lightweight, edible, gluten-free, stainless steel water bottle.

🙂 We both looked at ourselves in the mirror a lot. She seemed to be checking out her poses. I was making sure my lip gloss hadn't worn off, obviously.

🙂 We were both super exotic—she got her yoga certification in Mexico, and I drink Corona from Mexico. Samers.

🙂 We were both dancers. My kind required a pole and a generous dose of ~~tequila~~ courage. Hers didn't. Big deal.

🙂 We both listened to our bodies, as she frequently reminded us to do. Her body told her to stretch more deeply. Mine told me to drink lattes, but sometimes I waited until the end of class to go get one.

🙂 We both spoke English, but she used weird words like *heart chakra, prana* and *Namaste.* I used normal English words like *Oww!, I can't breathe. Someone help me!!,* and *I think I'm bleeding!!*

Even though we were obviously cut from the same cloth, we did have tiny differences:

☞ She could do *Downward Facing Dog* and talk at the same time. I preferred just to talk.

☞ She had a sexy tattoo that ringed around her six-pack ~~show-off~~ abs. Pfft. I had elastic marks from my sensible panties that totally looked like a tattoo around my ~~muffin top~~ super awesome abs.

☞ She wore a funky toe ring. I ~~hope it cuts into her flesh and gets infected~~ didn't because I couldn't risk a toe infection since I'll be wearing open-toed sandals in the pageant obviously.

☞ Her yoga pants were made of recycled bottles and looked like a second skin and cost $170. I didn't even know there was a pants rule until I was asked to please leave and return when I was more 'appropriately dressed'. Blah. Blah. Blah.

☞ She could touch her knee to her buttocks while standing on her baby toe. I could easily touch my breasts to my knees just by standing still. Boom.

I got better with each class, and eventually people couldn't tell the difference between me and the instructor!! Literally I could hold the *Warrior* pose for the entire hour because my muscles ~~seized up and I was paralyzed~~ were so flexible! I hate to brag, but my posture is way better already, and I feel totally ready to sit for hours on the *Miss World* float without getting all cramped, thanks to my ~~three~~ yoga classes!

Hot Yoga for a Hottie

After totally mastering regular yoga, I did what I always do—I ~~quit~~ raised the bar, obviously, and signed up for hot yoga. Firstly, it's like playing a game of *Twister* on the sun, and, secondly, it helps you to become total-ly ~~unconscious~~ flexible. Plus, it gets rid of nasty toxins and all signs of ~~life~~ stress. Sign me up.

As far as I'm concerned when the word 'hot' is in front of the word 'yoga' there's a reason for it. Before my first class, I perfected the Smoky Cat Eye with three shades of plum eye shadow, squeezed into my skinny jeans, and got some ~~liposuction~~ highlights. ~~Seven hours later,~~ I was ready for hot yoga!

When I arrived, I looked super hot, but my totally weird classmates didn't get the memo that hot yoga was for hot people. They were sprawled all over the floor in ridiculous looking shorts and wrinkled, sleeveless cotton tops. Get this—some of them didn't even have make-up on!!! Total freaks right? I ~~don't~~ regret blurting out, "Google 'hot' for once in your life!! You look like a bunch of has-beens lying around with your dull highlights!!" Whatever. As I strutted my stuff over to the mats, apparently my wedge-heeled, T-strap sandals were 'too loud' and 'unsafe' so the instructor asked me to remove them. Wow. Classic jealousy.

She then told us to lie on our mats. It was 450° and within thirty sec-onds my Smoky Cat Eye had melted into a *Hepatitis C-Raccoon Eye*. I lay down on my back and let the blanket of heat ~~suffocate~~ cover me. After two minutes, I was gasping for air, and my blood pressure completely stopped working. I tried to make eye contact with the woman beside me to ask her if this was normal, but her family had gathered around her to say good-bye, so I left them alone. By the time the instructor started class, I had lost fifteen pounds of water and was 'this close' to getting a complimentary IV drip (included in the monthly fee), but I powered through by slipping into a light ~~coma~~ sleep.

The yogi started by introducing herself and instructing us to raise our hand if we needed anything during the class. I shouted, "I can't even raise my eyebrows much less my hand!!" Ha! Ha! Kidding! It was in my head—I was too weak to speak obviously. Next, she did a head count so she could see how many she might lose from heat exhaustion by the end of class—very professional I thought.

We started with deep breathing. I kept inhaling my own perspiration, which led to coughing fits, which led to chest compressions by some random guy claiming to be a doctor, which is what every guy who does 'chest compressions' on me says. Nice line, guys, but I'm onto you!! Ha! Ha!

After the compressions, I don't mind saying I dazzled everyone with my favorite pose, *Downward Facing Dog*. It's an upside down 'V' with a bird's-eye view of your undercarriage. Our instructor told us the blood flow to your face and brain combined with the blistering room temperature will give you a ~~blood clot~~ youthful, dewy glow. Last time I checked you could get that same glow from L'Oreal Lumi Magique foundation.

The next pose was called *Happy Baby*. As soon as I heard the word, 'baby' I instantly relaxed, wailed, and begged for a snack. How was I supposed to know it meant to lie on your back, grab your big toes and rock side to side like a super childish toddler? I ended up liking that pose and stayed in it for the rest of the class—just rocking and sucking my thumb. This turned into a much-needed nap. I woke up when I heard the ~~ambulance sirens~~ instructor whisper, *Namaste*.

Who even cares that I didn't get my money's worth because I only did two poses before falling asleep? Unlike a few unlucky souls (sympathies to the families), I managed to get out alive. I felt horrible for tripping over the makeshift memorial of stainless steel water bottles, but every gal for herself, right?

I crawled to the change room and went straight to the mirror and what I saw will haunt me until my last regal breath—my hair was stuck to my head, my plum eye-shadow dripped down my cheeks, and my face oozed with all the toxins I had gotten rid of. I no longer looked totally hot. What was the point of this if I couldn't walk out the door and feel paparazzi-ready?? I learned an important lesson that day—hot yoga is for people who have no qualms about looking ugly. Besides, I checked the handbook and according to *Page 70, Section D, Subsection B1: Miss World need not be flexible, but she must be super hot.*

146

Section 7

Staying Totally ~~Not~~ Hot and Paparazzi-Ready! Comes with a ~~Mental~~ Price Tag

Being Stunning is Super Exhausting

Don't be jealous, but I received an amazing compliment from a colleague! She's twelve ~~weeks~~ years younger than I am, but she thought we were the same age. Imagine. Just for saying that, I gave her CNIB guide dog a treat. She asked what I did to hide my age. I responded, "Nothing really" and batted my ~~false~~ eyelashes. The truth is being stunning is literally exhausting. I'm working overtime to stay fit and gorgeous for the pageant, but it's getting harder by the minute. In case you're wondering how I do it, here are a few of my best kept secrets. You're totally welcome.

☻ Go for waxing on a regular basis. Nothing says youth like a soft ~~beardless~~ face. Make sure you don't overlook your nose and ear hair. Oh really? You don't have hair there do you? Well aren't you just a hairless wonder to behold? Pffft.

☻ Invest in a good ~~spanking~~ pair of Spanx. They squeeze everything into place, making you look super ~~blue from not being able to breathe~~ slim and awesome. In fact, I'm currently looking for bikini Spanx.

☻ Use an anti-ageing exfoliant. It will leave your skin refreshed and glowing. The bloody scars from all that scrubbing should fade in no time.

☻ Drink lots of water and ~~vodka gimlets~~ green tea. It will give you supple skin and good ~~times~~ circulation even though it tastes like total crap.

☻ Watch your diet. Avoid dairy, wheat, and anything that ~~tastes good~~ contains sugar. Fill up on anti-~~depressants~~ oxidants. They will help to keep diseases at bay even though all I want is to look super hot (Insert sizzling sound). Disease. Schimease.

☻ Use a rich, moisturizing night cream. It should contain Vitamin C, collagen, and ~~caulking~~ rose oil for youthful-looking results. I find this works best after a facelift, obviously.

☻ Go on a ~~bender~~ cleanse. It eliminates ~~stress~~ toxins and promotes ~~denial~~ glowing skin. It also makes you super hungry, so don't do what I did and eat a bucket of KFC the next day because it totally undid the benefits of the cleanse thingy.

☻ Cover your grey hair with the help of a good ~~paper bag~~ hairdresser. To avoid telling your husband you paid more for your hair than your car, take a secret trip to Paris until he worries about your whereabouts and forgets all about that hair snafu. It's totally worth it and is super fun!

No I'm not Hannibal Lecter, I'm spending my last dime on a face mask, that's what!

Boycott This Evil Product!

Sometimes it's just better to leave things alone. But because I'm super curious, I had to know what was going on with my chin and why I kept slicing my finger on it, I bought a cosmetic magnifying mirror thingy to get a closer look. It turned out to be the biggest mistake of my life and that includes the time I was hammered one night and bungee jumped off the house without a bungee cord.

I wish someone had warned me before I perched in front of this evil product because I wasn't mentally prepared for what stared back at me. I rubbed my hazel, gold-flecked eyes to see if it was real, and I haven't been the same since. It was hard enough to admit that I had a goatee, but was there really a family of squirrels nesting in it?!! OMG, what was going on down there?? I didn't know who to call first, the barber or the exterminator, so I poured myself a ~~bottle~~ glass of Cabernet Sauvignon and wept for those poor squirrels. They didn't stand a chance in that hairy mess. Bless them.

If you are not planning on competing in a beauty pageant, then my advice is to ~~smash to smithereens~~ boycott this evil product! Unfortunately, I have no choice because I'm in the beauty pageant circuit. According to the *Miss World* handbook, *Page 72, Section 3, Subsection 1B* goatees and beards are an absolute no-no for whatever ~~stupid~~ reason, so I've got to keep up on the pruning.

I wish I didn't have ~~a goatee~~ to share this information with you, but, if I can save just one person from the super devastating nightmare I experienced, I've got to give it to you straight. Save yourself and read below before purchasing one.

Do not use this product if you experience one or more of the following conditions: you have low blood pressure; you have a heart condition; you are prone to fainting spells; you are close to a knife drawer; you are prone to hysterical outbursts; you are close to a knife sharpener; you are prone to depression; you are fully conscious; you are alive; you think you look good; or you are happy. Make an emergency appointment with your ~~esthetician~~ doctor if any of these conditions arise while you are using a magnifying mirror.

The Bloody Red Blotches Sure Made Me Miss my Beard!

Spoiler alert—I get super enraged when I put my faith in "beauty experts" and end up with botched haircuts, pedicures, and wax jobs, but I keep it bottled up. For instance, I managed to block out what I'd seen in the evil magnifying mirror until I noticed kids in the mall following me and giving me their Christmas lists and asking if my beard was real. It wasn't even December. ~~Idiots~~.

Something had to be done, so I found an esthetician's number on the bathroom stall at Burger King and made an appointment for that afternoon. Bonus—she wasn't busy! Boom. When I arrived at her ~~dungeon~~ office, I tried not to hear the screams coming from the woman who went before me as I told myself the vat of bubbling wax wouldn't hurt a bit against my tender skin.

I had almost convinced myself that I could live with a beard when the esthetician called me in. She took one look at me and asked, "Beard oil or weed whacker?" I can't say I loved her ~~stupid~~ attitude, and I very politely set her straight, "I'll have you know that ~~I was hairless before #$%ing menopause~~ European women have hair everywhere!"

What came next haunts me to this day. She lathered super hot wax from my eyebrows to my neck. With no ~~conscience~~ hesitation whatsoever, she butted out her cigarette and ripped three layers off my stunning face! When I came to, I could smell burning flesh mingled with the smelling salts she used to bring me back to life. Fun fact—my therapist thinks my hatred of candles can be traced back to this devastating experience.

It was over in five minutes, thank God. I was in a daze, but I managed to find the strength to ~~kick her hard in the shins~~ speak, "I smell blood." She pretended not to hear—probably on the advice of her lawyer. Then she handed me a mirror to show me where I'd need skin grafting. The spot where my beard used to rest was now a blotchy, oozing mess. WTF would I tell the pageant organizers when they caught wind of this?!

As always, my amazing personality took over. I didn't want to make a fuss, so I graciously asked the esthetician if she would like me to sign something for her. Literally not recognizing me as *Miss Nackawic 1981*, she said, "You can sign your credit card receipt. That'll be $50." I responded, "~~See you in court, you miserable piece of s***!~~ Thanks for ~~destroying my chance at the title~~ everything—I can't wait to see how my face looks when it scabs over!"

I'm totally torn. Part of me would like to be more assertive when so-called experts screw me over, but beauty queens are supposed to be mature and nice, so maybe now isn't the time to get all aggressive. One day I'll get it all out. Juuuusst you wait. Ha! Ha!

A Cut Below the Rest

Call me crazy, but I want my hairdresser to have experience, confidence, and ~~brain activity~~ styling know-how. I am disgusted when she asks which color or style I would like. Shouldn't **she** know what would look best on me? I don't tell my dentist how to fill my tooth; I don't tell my mechanic how to grease my engine (Yes I do. Wink. Wink.); and I certainly don't tell my surgeon how high to lift my butt cheeks. I leave it up to the experts. I recently messed with an inexperienced hairdresser, and I pray to God she ~~dies alone face down in a gutter~~ gets some upgrading.

My regular hairdresser had injured her hands and was off work for a month. Boo! hoo! What kind of person abandons her clients just because of a few ~~#$%ing~~ misshapen fingers? My normally soft, shiny locks were in bad shape, so I had no choice but to take a ~~month off work and stay in bed~~ chance on my hairdresser's young and inexperienced replacement.

I asked the receptionist who the toddler running around with scissors was and almost passed out when she told me it was the new hairdresser. When said hairdresser told me she had graduated from college that morning, I felt totally ~~terrified~~ better. After she gushed about her awesome boyfriend and revealed her latest piercing, I said, "Screw up my hair and I'll gut you like a pig. Just a trim, little one." It seemed simple enough, but her endless questions totally freaked me out!

What are bangs?
What do the 'H' and 'C' on this tap thingy mean?
Should I hold the scissors by the circles or the pointy part?

After fifty minutes of her destroying any hope I had of winning *Miss World*, I taught her how to turn the hydraulic chair around so I could face the mirror. I didn't ~~hit her hard~~ like the cut at all, and this was the week I had a hired a professional photographer for my *Miss World* photo -op!! I had no choice but to take a selfie and text it to my hypochondriac hairdresser with this message: *Look at this mess on my head!! See what happens when you take time off?? How can you even live with yourself? PS If I don't win Miss World, it will be totally your fault. Good luck trying to live with that!*

Booty Call

Though I'm still super ~~wrinkly~~ hot, midlife has totally messed up my brain! I can't make decisions. I overthink the tiniest details: Feed the homeless or adopt seven children? Get Botox or a nose job? Then there are the totally *agonizing* choices, like which winter boots to buy.

Because Canadian winters last roughly one hundred years, I ~~pray the Miss World pageant is in California~~ am forced to wear unflattering bulky coats, throw ~~tantrums~~ spray tan parties, and go on week-long ~~rampages~~ shopping excursions for the perfect boots. It's hard to be me.

The boots had to scream *Miss World,* but hypothermia was out of the question because I also had to protect all ten toes for the pageant's catwalk, so they had to be warm. I had no choice but to rent a U-Haul in case I found, like, a thousand contenders. It was easier to bring them home to try on, and Phil ~~hates~~ adores it when I ask his opinion. Win/win!

Phil was stoked when he heard the beeping of the U-Haul as I backed into the driveway because he thought I'd bought us a backhoe. Ha! Ha! What a goofball. His disappointment turned into total grumpiness after I nicked the house with the U-Haul. Oops! When I lugged all those boots into the living room, his eyes bugged out, and he started sighing and mumbling to himself. Wow—don't say I said so, but that guy can be super moody.

The first pair I tried on were a black, high heel, knee-length, pointy-toe, calf-squeezing number, a half size too small. When the swelling and bleeding became too much, I used a sleek ~~firefighter~~ crowbar to haul me out of them. Then there was the chocolate brown Italian suede ankle boots with chunky heels that were lined with authentic Italian baby swans. They were to die for and totally comfortable, but my husband wouldn't agree to a ~~third~~ second mortgage. Fine. Be moody *and* selfish.

After two weeks of hardcore shopping, I was down to twenty-six pairs of boots. It was an awesome opportunity for my husband and me to bond and share opinions. I asked him, "~~Why didn't you become a doctor so I could keep all of them???~~ Which pair do you like best? Be honest." I could tell he was happy for me, but he didn't want to commit to an opinion in case it caused a divorce tension. He just remained neutral and said, "Do you really need new boots?" I didn't speak to him for a month after he said those terrible words.

I literally couldn't decide!! The weather was getting colder, and the thought of me on the catwalk with seven toes motivated me to not give up. After spending hours poring over Pinterest, I decided to go with what Kate Middleton was wearing on her feet when she left the palace on that cold day in December. We're both royalty after all, so, if she can have designer boots, so can I. Boom.

I went to a high-end shoe store and asked a sales clerk to fetch me knee-high, black leather riding boots with 1¼ inch heels, 2-inch wide buckle strap accents, alpaca lining, and a full-length silver zipper. She gave me the weirdest look and said, "This ain't LA, honey." After she said those horrible words, she did something unforgivable—she showed me a clearance rack with the boots that were left since it was now March. Clearance!! How *dare* she?? Obviously she didn't know who I was and would be sorry one day when I was *Miss You Know Who*!!!

Apparently Kate Middleton shops in London because, for the life of me, I could not find her boots! Whatever. The good news is I finally made a decision—I would just sit out the winter and keep my feet super supple and warm for the bikini portion. After all, I'll be damned if I'm wearing a closed-toe sandal like I did for *Miss Nackawic*. No way. Put *that* in your clearance rack pipe and smoke it, Ms. Sales Clerk from Hell.

The Nice Police Officer Told Me About Qigong

It's no secret I've been living for one thing and one thing only, but I'll be honest—once I turned ~~50~~ 40 'something', I seriously wondered if this dream that was slipping through my ~~liver-spotted~~ fingers would ever come true. Night after night, I would lie in bed, with my vision board and tiara, wondering why this goal seemed super ~~impossible~~ hard to achieve! It's not like I don't have any beauty queen experience for the lovofgod. News flash: I was *Miss Nackawic 1981*!! Duh.

I knew I had to get a grip after the shopping cart incident at Costco, even though it was totally blown out of proportion. Frig—those massive shopping carts are impossible to drive and please define 'rammed into at high speed'. Also, I hardly think it necessitated a police escort to my car.

The nice police officer sensed my ~~white hot rage~~ restlessness and told me about a Qigong (Chee Kung) class that was being offered at a local gym. After I filled out the boring forms at the police station, I drove ~~60 km over the speed limit~~ home to Google *Qigong*. It was described as walking meditation and a form of gentle exercise made up of repetitive movements—it sounded super relaxing. Plus, it sounded so easy you could do it in a skin tight evening gown draped with a sash. Sign me up!

After handing over my $150 cheque to the instructor, I was ready to focus more on the journey than the outcome and become totally zen and mindful. To prove it, I said, "This class was supposed to start three minutes ago!! What's the ~~#$%-ing~~ hold up??" The instructor put her finger to her lips and rudely shushed me. She told us to take deep breaths and listen to our breathing to keep us focused. Booooring!

We learned our first move—*Flying Cloud Hands*. It felt weird and lame at first, but I got super good at it and even considered using it for my *Miss World* talent. Then I remembered to be mindful and brought myself back to the present moment…or was it a familiar, but terrible sound that brought me back? Yes. Now I remember. It *was* a sound…of fully grown and also totally weird adults having what our instructor referred to as releases, which is Sanskrit for burping and farting. I was literally horrified because these so-called releases were a total *no no* in the beauty pageant circuit according to *Page 49, Section C, Subsection 1A* of the handbook!

According to our instructor, 'releases' are encouraged to get rid of bad 'qi' (chee). By the sound and smell of things in there, my guess is there was also some bad cheese. I felt like I was in an Irritable Bowel support group meeting. To show my support, I lifted my leg and let one rip because I have such a need to fit in.

Because I wanted to stay ~~out of jail~~ on track with living in the moment, I went back the following week. We learned a new move called *Swaying the Head and Swinging the Tail*, which apparently activates the energy of the kidneys and unblocks worry, anxiety, and ~~your bowels~~ distress. I was really getting into it. My eyes were closed, I was totally mindful, and I was swinging my booty like no one was watching until I realized that *Ms. Refried Beans* to my left had officially unblocked her kidneys *and bowel*. I hadn't heard such horrible noises coming from a pair of pants since Phil released his qi after supper.

This is gonna sound super crazy, but, when anyone in the class burped and farted, the instructor smiled and said, "Wonderful! You're getting rid of bad qi. Don't be afraid to release. There's ~~toilet paper~~ hope for everyone!" In my house, when my menfolk 'release their qi', I gag, wave my hand in front of my nose and tell them to go to ~~Australia~~ the #$%ing bathroom.

By the third class, the releases were so loud, I couldn't ~~ignore my urge to ram a Costco shopping cart into someone~~ even think. I was getting *Flying Cloud Hands* mixed up with *Swaying the Head and Swinging the Tail*. I looked like Beyonce (but hotter obviously) and Stevie Wonder as I twerked and swayed like no one was watching. I was living in the present, but the present totally sucked! I wanted to go back to living in the future and staring at my vision board. Qigong was ~~for total losers~~ not for me, obviously.

I know the nice police officer had good intentions, but, if I want to listen to someone burp and fart for an hour, I just have to go into my TV room after a meal. Plus, living in the moment is a total a waste of time. If I don't think about my awesome future as *Miss World*, how in God's name will it happen?

Qigong was a total bust, obviously. I needed something else to settle my mind, and I found it by accident one hot summer afternoon. While on a bike ride, I ran into two ~~trees~~ girls running a lemonade stand. I pulled over for a sample and to shoot the breeze with them:

Hey, girls, if this business is under the table, so help me God I will report you to Revenue Canada.

I'll give you a buck for an iced Venti chai latte and hurry it up.

You got somethin' a little stronger back there? Wink. Wink. Nudge. Nudge.

Despite my friendly and awesome personality, I received nothing but blank stares—kids are so weird these days. I hopped on my bike ~~after they called 911~~ and got to thinking I could use some extra money because my *Miss World* expenses were racking up. Why should those non-verbal kids corner the market? The harder I pedaled, the harder I mentally tweaked my business plan—I knew what *I* wanted in the middle of a hot afternoon, obviously, but would mojitos actually sell?? Of course they would. Duh. It was foolproof.

I wanted my mojito stand to be professional, but I only had five minutes because it was already 29°C out, and my future customers were hot and thirsty. Here's what ~~my marketing department~~ I came up with:

MOHJITOS 4 SALE: LIMIT- 5(ish) PER CUSTOMER

Advertising was next. How would I let the people know I was selling rum in my driveway? Twitter obviously—@missnackawic1981 *Ramp up ur mojo with a mojito! Mix it and they will come. Cash only @145 Hills Rd #thirsty #much?*

Boom. I was a businesswoman!! Eeeeeeee!! I mixed my ingredients in a large bowl without measuring. Pfft. Not everything has to be perfect. It was totally my duty to make sure the ~~straight~~ rum drinks were worth ~~ten~~ fifteen bucks a pop, so I had no choice but to sample. My paranoid husband asked, "What in the name of God are you doing?" I said, "I'll have you know you are married to an awesome businesswoman, and I do not appreciate your tone."

After my second sampling (Judge yourself!), I rummaged downstairs for a table for my mojito stand. I found an old TV tray, and Boom. It was show time! Apparently a business degree is a total waste of time and money, because I was doing just fine without one.

As with all new businesses, one can't expect immediate success:

Business Hours: Right Friggin' Now
Form a Single Line, Please

Where the #$%! is everyone? Fine. Suffer in the heat, losers. See if I care.

*@missnackawic1981Mojitos 4 sale! Credit cards
now accepted #limited #supply*

Issh hot out here. I'm shleepy.

Oooh...Mishter big tough poleesh offisher shut me down. Pffft. Permit. Schmermit.

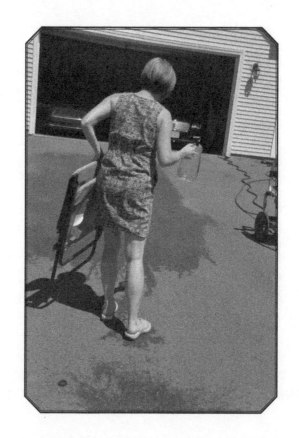

Dear Neighboursh: I hope you die of thirsht. Literally.

I woke up the next day with ~~dry heaves~~ a much better attitude. I figured out why my mojitos didn't sell. The price point was bang on, I was super approachable, and the drinks were perfect, but in the end what killed me was that I hadn't done anything to separate myself from other driveway vendors. Duh. I needed a gimmick and ~~as I was bent over the toilet bowl~~ it came to me—I would add a karaoke machine with the mojitos. People obviously want to belt it into a mic after a mojito or two. I'd even sing a duet with them if they begged me hard enough.

I learned so much from this awesome experience—it often takes more than five ~~minutes~~ years to grow your business; police officers can be heavy-handed for no good reason; and most importantly, ~~drinking mojitos~~ being engaged in something can add joy to your middle years. So go ahead and try something that scares you silly. I did and it totally worked. Obviously.

You Guys Owe Me Some Friggin' Money!

I need to know where to submit my expense claims immediately, especially since my mojito stand wasn't as profitable as I had hoped. As you know, I have submitted several airbrushed photos of myself along with my resume. If you think for one minute that I wake up in the morning looking like that, you're insane! It takes ~~weeks~~ hours and ~~thousands~~ hundreds of dollars to get that natural, Ivory-girl glow. Also, please don't tell my husband, but I had to quit my job because my wrinkles and age spots take so much more time to cover these days. I just couldn't get to work before noon, and apparently my 'contract' states that my day begins at 8 a.m. Well, *pardon me* for having dreams bigger than merely keeping a roof over my head! Frig that.

Since I'm no longer employed, and I have literally *no clue* when I'm going to take the crown and cash prize, I'm asking for what is rightfully mine. Following is an itemized list of the products I require to be able to compete in *Miss World*, complete with prices:

🌸 Serum for deep moisturizing→$75 (I'm certainly not using the cheap stuff at this stage in the game. No way.)

🌸 Eye cream for delicate skin around the eye→$50 (I'm certainly not using heavy cream on a delicate part of my face. No way.)

🌸 Exfoliant→$35 (I'm certainly not moisturizing over dead skin cells. As if.)

🌸 Tweezers→$25 (I'm certainly not using cheap tweezers and the handbook says no beards, moustaches or goatees. Your rules, not mine!)

🌸 Eyelash conditioner→$90 (I'm certainly not entering a pageant of this caliber with skimpy eyelashes!! Good Lord.)

🌸 Teeth whitening strips→$60 (See Miss World Handbook *Page 74, Section D, Subsection B3: No contestant will have yellow teeth.*)

🌸 Highlights→$150 (Duh.)

🌸 Hair products→$225 Conditioner, serum, paste (We all know I didn't win *Miss New Brunswick* due in part to split ends. Fool me once…)

☻ Body cream→$35 (I'm tired of people using my arms as sandpaper)

☻ Crowbar→$45 (How else am I going to get into that Spanx on pageant night?)

I took it upon myself to tally it for you and the grand total is $5,891.33. Shocking ~~that I graduated~~ right?! Well now, you know why I'm 'this close' to being homeless! Honestly, at times I wonder if this is all worth it—all this money and time I'm spending could be literally for nothing! Psych!!! Ha! Ha! Of course it's worth it! Duh. All I need is a bit more money to tide me over until the big day. So, if you'll just pop that cheque in the mail, I'll be good to go! Please don't dilly dally as I have a ~~face lift~~ hair appointment tomorrow. Blessings!

Dear Ms. World Pageant Organizers

April 1st, 2018

Dear Miss World Pageant Organizers:

My therapist said I should write you a letter to show how angry and disappointed I am and then burn it. But I couldn't find my lighter, so I decided to send it—you won't read it anyway since you're obviously illiterate. Furthermore, the only thing burning around here is the white hot rage deep in my belly.

I've devoted my entire life to you. I've written letter after letter; I've waxed myself into a bloody pulp; I've stayed in ~~a pear~~ shape; I've raised two super awesome boys while honing my entertaining/cooking/decorating skills, and for what?!? For crickets, silence, nothing, that's what. You continue to ignore me, but now hear this: Once a beauty queen, always a beauty queen. I'll find you and your ~~mother #$%ing~~ pageant if it's the last thing I do!! If you'd learn how to read for once in your life, you'd see from this lengthy tome that I'm almost ~~100 #$%ing years old~~ past the age when a woman can walk across a stage in a bikini and the perfect open-toe sandal with any shred of dignity. I watch the pageant on TV, and I'm not an idiot! I can tell that the winners are a tiny bit younger than I am. I'm not sure how many laser resurfacing treatments a person can have before her skin just disappears into thin air, but that doesn't seem to keep you up at night the way it does me. I don't know how you live with yourselves knowing you've left me hanging for thirty-six years. Thirty-six ~~mother #$%ing~~ years!! Well, you might want to learn how to read because you'll soon be getting an afferdavete (How do *you* spell it, Einsten??) that says I'm taking you to court. You heard me. I plan to sue you for personal mental injury. That's right. You've mentally injured me and now it's payback.

Sincerely,

Miss Nackawic 1981

PS I would have made the most beautiful *Miss World*. Sorry for your loss!

166

Three Weeks Later. . .

OMG! OMG! OMG! Tough love works!! Check out the letter I *finally* received from the Miss World Pageant Organizers. EEEEEE!! Patience is a virtue and dreams do come true, even if they take thirty-six years. Two words: I'm in! Boom.

Colleen Landry
731 Royalty Lane
La La Land

April 14, 2018

RE: Disciplinary hearing regarding Colleen Landry AKA Miss Nackawic 1981

Dear Ms. Landry:

In response to a letter of complaint against you by **Miss World Pageant Organizing Committee**, charges were made to the Disciplinary Committee.

The complaint alleges that you **repeatedly harassed and verbally stalked members of the Miss World Pageant Organizing Committee over a period of thirty-six years.**

You are charged with a violation of Code CDR 3.

The hearing has been scheduled for **November 15, 2018**. If you do not appear, the hearing will proceed without you. In the event you are disciplined, you will be provided with information related to appeal.

Sincerely,

UR Skrewd, LLB

Corporate Attorney for Miss World Pageant Inc.

April 21st, 2018

Dear Ms. World Pageant Organizers:

I can't express how excited I am that you finally got back to me!! *As if* I would 'not appear' in court! You're kidding, right?? I'm literally vibrating at the thought of meeting you guys for reals. It has felt totally one-sided for thirty-six years, but my vision board actually worked!! You have been listening after all! Forgive me for being super emotional but when a dream comes true, a girl has the right to blubber a bit. I promise to wear waterproof mascara at the hearing!!

Also I plan to impress you guys so hard you'll probably want to ~~incarcerate~~ crown me right on the spot. Ha! Ha! (Bring the tiara in case, k?)

See you soon! Air kisses! OMG! OMG!

Sincerely (relieved and grateful),

Colleen Landry
Miss Nackawic 1981

PS What should I wear??

PPS Will you guys be covering my court expenses? xoxo

Two Weeks Later. . .

May 5th, 2018

Dear Miss World Pageant Organizers:

Me again!! I'm still totally stoked except for one thing—you forgot to answer my question about court expenses! I know the hearing isn't until November but my greedy lawyer is charging me a horrible amount of money because apparently if I represent myself in court I'll end up in the ~~slammer~~ hot seat. Pfft.

I suppose if I have to clear this one last hurdle for the title I'll do it but holy frig!!!! I've already sold two evening gowns and drained our boys' university fund for a grand total of $1057 which didn't even cover the first afferdavete I sent you guys! How in God's name will I come up with the other million thousands I owe Mr. Smarty Pants Lawyer?? Mojito stands don't work, obviously, but I'll come up with something, promise!

Sincerely,

Colleen Landry
Miss Nackawic 1981

PS Good thing I work well under pressure because now my husband is talking legal mumbo jumbo too because of that university fund I drained. I wish I had more support around here, but whatever.

Five Weeks Later. . .

June 10th, 2018

Dear Miss World Pageant Organizers:

OMG! OMG! Guess what, you guys?? I literally just won a big time author award for the second Camelia Airheart book I wrote with ~~Beth and Odette~~ all by myself!!! It's called *Take off to Tantramar* and it won best picture book in New Brunswick ~~the entire universe~~!!!

Winning this super amazing award gave me an idea—I'm going to write a bestseller and make millions, probably by next week!! They say to write what you know so my bestseller will be about what it's like to be *Miss Nackawic 1981*—the highs, the lows, the endless struggles etc.—God knows I've lived it. Furthermore, I'll be able to easily pay my greedy lawyer and still have seven billion dollars left over. Boom.

My only concern is this—with this latest development, will I even have time to be *Miss World 2018*?? Psych!!! Ha! Ha! I'll make time, you guys!!

See you in court—I literally can't wait to get this thing rolling…finally!!!

Sincerely blessed and beyond excited,

Colleen Landry
Miss Nackawic 1981

PS How many copies of my upcoming bestseller should I put you down for? I'm sure it will be on the shelves by November. It's already June. Duh. Books are super easy to write.

PPS I can give you a special price because we're practically BFFs now—I plan to charge $30/book. How about I bring 15 copies for you and you can pay me the $500 when I see you at our little court meeting.

PPPS Oooops!!! My bad. I did the math wrong. Duh. Sorry…you owe me $545.27. Please bring a cheque and make it out to *Miss World 2018*. Boom.

My Publisher Said I Had to Put in Some Acknowledgements. Pfft

FYI, I think everyone should thank me for writing this super hilarious book but apparently I'm supposed to thank others. Pfft. Whatever.

Thank you to my cherished royal family—my awesome husband, Phil, and our totally amazing loinfruits, Alex and Max, for ~~unknowingly~~ generously allowing me to use them as material and for bearing the heavy burden of royalty—they've handled it with grace, dignity and total ~~oblivion~~ poise. They're literally the best!

Thank you to my super supportive friends and relations who always laughed ~~at me behind my back~~ in all the right places, left encouraging comments on my *One Hot Flashin' Mama* blog posts, and gave me helpful writing tips as well as the ~~overblown~~ confidence I needed to write this international bestseller.

Thank you to my totally excellent publisher, Kate Merlin from Chocolate River Publishing, for her ~~sometimes uncalled for~~ insightful feedback. She'll miss my nightly phone calls, "Kate, surely you can add one more photo of me!! You're not even trying!" Thank you to Margaret Hanson-Clarke for her totally ~~picky~~ awesome edits. ~~Continuity-schmontinuity.~~ And thanks to Chris Helgason for the amazing cover art—I look ~~much better~~ stunning as an animation.

Thank you to the *Miss Nackawic 1981* judges because, without them, I might just be some washed up housewife/teacher/mother but because of them I'm ~~not~~ so much more!!

There would be no book without Nackawic—my sweet little hometown where as a beautiful, precocious child I'd bike with my bestie to my Grammy and Grampy's house for raw rhubarb (you heard me) and seventeen~~ish~~ homemade molasses cookies; where my friends and I would play outside until we heard the 8 p.m. mill whistle—our curfew; where my friends and I would gather at the arena on weekends to cheer for our high school hockey team ~~by throwing bottles on the ice~~; and where I became the ~~delusional~~ beauty queen I was destined to be (in 1981). Thanks for the memories, Nackawic!

Photo and Artwork Credits

Cover artwork © Chris Helgason

Photo Page 5 reprinted with permission of the Miss Nackawic Pageant organizers

Backcover author photo ©Sharon MacPhee

Page 33 Family photo © Rachelle Richard-Leger and reprinted with permission

Pages 77-79 Photos of Jak ©Kathy Jessop and reprinted with permission